LOUIS RIEL

The Rebel
and
The Hero

Hartwell Bowsfield

"We must never forget that, in the long run,
a democracy is judged by the way the majority treats the minority. Louis Riel's battle
is not yet won."   PIERRE ELLIOTT TRUDEAU

Toronto
OXFORD UNIVERSITY PRESS
1971

TO MAY BOWSFIELD

Soc
F
1063
B65

The maps are by Ronald G. Curtis, C.C.

ISBN 0—19—540182—4

2 3 4 5 6 — 6 5 4 3 2

Printed in Canada by John Deyell Limited

Contents

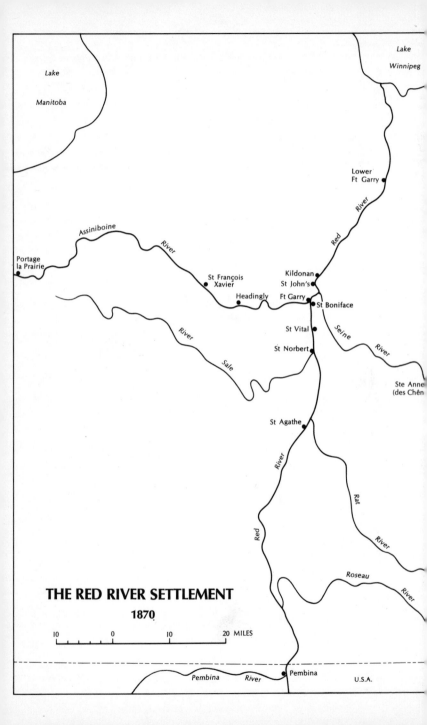

THE RED RIVER SETTLEMENT

1870

Lake Winnipeg

Lake Manitoba

Lower Ft Garry

Red River

Assiniboine River

Portage la Prairie

St François Xavier

Kildonan

St John's

Headingly

Ft Garry

St Boniface

Seine River

St Vital

Ste Anne (des Chên

River Sale

St Norbert

St Agathe

Red River

Rat River

Roseau River

10   0   10   20 MILES

Pembina River

Pembina

U.S.A.

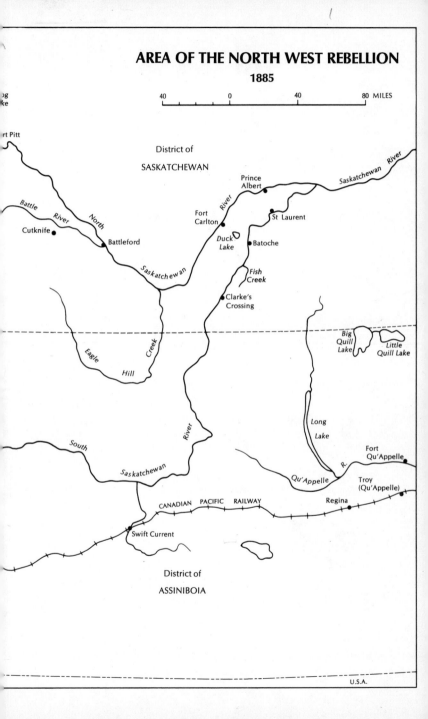

AREA OF THE NORTH WEST REBELLION
1885

40   0   40   80 MILES

rt Pitt

District of
SASKATCHEWAN

Prince
Albert

Saskatchewan River

Battle River North

Cutknife

Fort
Carlton

River

St Laurent

Battleford

Saskatchewan

Duck
Lake

Batoche

Fish
Creek

Clarke's
Crossing

Big
Quill
Lake

Little
Quill Lake

Eagle

Creek

Hill

River

Long
Lake

South

Fort
Qu'Appelle

Saskatchewan

R.

Qu'Appelle

Troy
(Qu'Appelle)

CANADIAN   PACIFIC   RAILWAY

Regina

Swift Current

District of
ASSINIBOIA

U.S.A.

Illustrations

Preface

The rise and fall of Louis Riel (1844-85) covered only fifteen years in the story of the Canadian West, yet he is one of the few people in our history who command almost as much interest today as they did in their own time. He was the central figure in a tragedy, the result of excesses he resorted to when confronted by the bigotry and incomprehension of his opponents. The tragedy unfolds inevitably, at a time when religious and racial feelings in Canada were passionate and narrow and political opportunism was ruthless. It has so caught the imagination of modern Canadians that Riel has become a folk hero—a fitting subject for drama and opera.

Both in his own time and after, Riel inspired hatred and idolatry, admiration and contempt. If feelings about him were mixed, Riel himself was filled with ambiguities and apparent contradictions. He was a man of intelligence and authority who was mentally unstable; a reasonable protester against legitimate grievances who turned fanatic and dictatorial; a gentle man whose name became associated with violence even though he himself never took up arms; a simple man of great personal appeal who developed grandiose pretensions as a spiritual and political leader; a visionary and an erratic religious mystic who inspired unquestioning faith in the Métis people. He had a burning sense of injustice and of his God-given mission to remove it, but only a confused understanding of how best to go about his work. Though his act of resistance to Canada in 1870 and the halfhearted rebellion of 1885 were quickly crushed, the consequences for the West and the country as a whole were immense. Riel has rightly been called the Father of Manitoba. The creation of that province in 1870 ensured the fulfilment of the transcontinental destiny of the young Confederation.

These events can be examined in terms of the religious and racial conflict existing between Quebec and Ontario, or of the clash between primitive and civilized societies. They can also be related to the contention that exists today between the two main language groups in the Canadian federation. But however they are viewed, there remains at the centre the compelling figure of Louis Riel—a hero and a martyr to some, a pathetic traitor and a murderer to others. A truer and fuller characterization emerges as we consider the life and times of a man in whom simplicity, megalomania, nobility, and madness were all combined.

1
Young Riel

Louis Riel was born on October 27, 1844 in a log house on the Seine River, near present-day Winnipeg. On the same day, at the cathedral of St Boniface, he was baptized by Bishop Provencher, who had married his parents the year before. He was named after his father.

Louis was the eldest of eleven children born to Julie Lagimodière, a deeply religious woman who had grown up in the West, in the Red River Settlement. Her husband Louis was also born in the West, at Ile à la Cross (Sask.), of a mother who was part Chipewyan. However, Louis Riel the Elder grew up at Berthier in Lower Canada (Quebec), where his family moved in 1822 when he was five. He attended school there and learned the trade of a wool carder. When he was twenty-one he joined the Hudson's Bay Company and worked at Rainy River. He left the Company's service in 1842 and joined the Oblate order to become a priest; but he gave up this intention a few months later and went back once and for all to the West. He was given some land in the Red River Settlement and the next year married Julie Lagimodière.

To understand the career of the younger Riel, we have to know something of the prairies in the first half of the nineteenth century; the environment of the settled area

9

around present-day Winnipeg where Louis Riel grew up; the conditions that for a long time made life in the Red River district uneasy and culminated in events that brought about Riel's rise to power among his people and his eventual destruction.

The Canadian West was first opened up in the eighteenth century by French-Canadian explorers and fur traders from Quebec. Many of these men took Indian women as wives, and the children of such marriages became known as Métis—people of mixed blood. Marriage to an Indian woman could be useful. From her the trader could learn an Indian language and through her an alliance could be made with her tribe, giving the trader a close and peaceful contact with the Indian people. This Indian connection served the French-Canadian traders well in their competition with the British-owned Hudson's Bay Company, for their intimate association with the tribes strengthened their influence over the Indians in keeping a good part of the fur trade in their own hands and out of the hands of the Company posts on Hudson Bay.

After the fall of New France in 1759, the French-Canadian fur trade with the Northwest came to an end. Trade passed into the hands of English, Scottish, and American merchants who moved into Montreal. The French-Canadian connection with the Northwest was never destroyed, however. The French language had been introduced. The existence of the Métis people was evidence that French-Canadian blood would remain. And the influence of the Roman Catholic Church, established by missionaries who accompanied the explorers and fur traders, was very much present. Through language, blood, and religion, then, a part of French Canada would always exist in the Northwest.

The new traders—called Pedlars by the Hudson's Bay Company men because they carried their trade goods directly into the Indian camps—took over the French-Canadian trade routes and methods. They made good use also of French-Canadian experience and ability by employing French Canadians as voyageurs, interpreters, and guides. As the Pedlars and their successors, the XY Company and the North West Company, extended their trade westward, up into the Mackenzie River basin and beyond the Rocky Mountains, they became more and more dependent on pemmican for their food. Made by mixing dried buffalo meat with melted fat, pemmican was plentiful and nourishing (though not at all tasty); it could be preserved for a long time; and it was easily transported. The Métis took on a special importance to the traders when they became suppliers of pemmican. Having learned the skills of the buffalo hunt from the Indians—for whom the buffalo had always been a source of food, clothing, and implements—the Métis became superb horsemen and easily surpassed the Indians in the hunt and in organizing a trade with which they soon became identified. As their special and useful role in prairie life began to develop, the Métis came to think of themselves as a recognizable group, which of course they were, being different from both the white man and the Indian. Their means of livelihood, the buffalo hunt, and their occasional skirmishes with the Sioux Indians had taught them to rely on organization, leadership, and discipline. The sense of "nationhood" they developed would have profound effects on the history of the West and especially on the life of Louis Riel.

The Métis became tools in the struggle for control of the western fur trade between the North West Company, centred in Montreal, and the British Hudson's Bay Company, which had acquired ownership of the Northwest (called Rupert's

Land) in 1670. In 1811 the Hudson's Bay Company granted Lord Selkirk, a Scottish colonizer, 116,000 square miles of land that became known as Assiniboia and he established a settlement at the junction of the Red and Assiniboine Rivers, where Winnipeg is today. By this time the district was important not for the furs it produced but as the principal source of provisions and pemmican vital to the fur trade. The men of the North West Company—the Nor'Westers—were convinced that the Selkirk Settlement on the Red River was a scheme of the Hudson's Bay Company, in which Selkirk was a stockholder, to wipe out their business. They set out to destroy the Settlement. Part of their plan involved the Métis, who were closely associated with the North West Company as buffalo hunters and were living in the area of the Settlement. The Nor'Westers encouraged the Métis's sense of pride, of being a separate people, and cultivated in them a feeling of grievance against the settlers, who, the Métis were told, had come to rob them of land that was rightfully theirs by virtue of their mothers' Indian blood.

At the end of August 1812, Miles Macdonell, the first Governor of Assiniboia, arrived with an advance party of twenty-three—the first Selkirk settlers. No sooner had they camped on the east bank of the Red River, opposite the North West Company's Fort Gibraltar, than a band of Métis horsemen rode up, dressed in war paint and feathers. They told Macdonell and his party that settlers were not welcome, that the land belonged to them, the Métis. This was the first of many confrontations between the Métis and the Red River settlers, all of them planned by the North West Company, who told the Métis that they must "clean their native soil of the intruder". These efforts were not completely successful, however. Though the settlers were harassed on two occasions to the point of leaving their settlement, they returned each time.

In June 1816, in the Massacre of Seven Oaks, Governor Robert Semple, Macdonell's successor, and twenty settlers and Hudson's Bay Company men were killed by Métis under the leadership of Cuthbert Grant, a halfbreed (he had a Scottish father). The remaining settlers left and went a few miles down the Red River. Lord Selkirk arrived at Red River the following summer and stayed for three months. By directing surveys, planning roads, bridges, and mill sites, he created what became the first agricultural settlement in the Northwest, and gave it a firm and permanent basis.

Partly through Selkirk's efforts two Roman Catholic priests, Father Provencher and Father Dumoulin, came to Red River in 1818 with about forty French-Canadian families. One of their first tasks was to begin consolidating the scattered groups of Métis near the forks of the Red and Assiniboine Rivers. A large settlement of about 500 Métis from just south of the American border at Pembina was gradually moved to St Boniface. This was completed by about 1823. Another Métis settlement was established along the Assiniboine River west of the forks at what became known as Grantown, named after Cuthbert Grant. At Grantown, later called St François Xavier, the Métis continued to live as buffalo hunters and as guardians of the main Settlement from the Sioux, the traditional enemies of the Indians of the Red River region—the Cree, the Saulteaux, and the Assiniboines. As guardians of the Settlement, the Métis found for themselves an important and useful role in the life of the Red River Settlement.

Once the enemies of the Settlement, the Métis were now its protectors. The change was assisted by the union of the

North West and Hudson's Bay Companies in 1821 and by the work of the priests who had come to live with the Métis. George Simpson, the energetic Governor of the Hudson's Bay Company territories in Canada, was satisfied that the Métis had been exploited by the North West Company in the fur-trade rivalry. He knew how useful the Métis could be both to the fur trade and to the Settlement. Cuthbert Grant, he wrote in 1822, "seems to have been entirely made a party tool of". Simpson brought Grant into the Hudson's Bay Company service and the Métis leader served first as a clerk in the Lower Red River District and in 1824 was given the responsibility of establishing the settlement at Grantown.

The Métis had made their peace with the Settlement but, unlike the Scottish and English halfbreeds and the Selkirk settlers, many of them were not content to give in completely to the routine duties of farming. The settled habits and comforts of an agricultural life were less attractive than the excitement of a buffalo hunt or a trip with fur traders to the far Northwest as guides or interpreters. Concentrating the Métis in settlements along the Red and Assiniboine Rivers was part of a program designed by Simpson to protect both the Settlement and the fur monopoly of the Hudson's Bay Company. "Unless early means are taken to bring them round to industrious habits and withdraw them from the plains," he wrote of the Métis in 1824, "I do most seriously apprehend that they will in due time be the destruction of the Colony." This fear had led him to recommend the establishment of Grantown and to bring the Métis from Pembina to St Boniface. Though Pembina was close to the buffalo grounds, it was in American territory, and Simpson feared that American fur traders might use the Métis to draw off furs from the Company's territories. He was concerned also that the Sioux, who looked upon the Métis at Pembina as intruders in their hunting grounds, might retaliate against the Red River Settlement.

Even while Simpson was attempting to insulate the Settlement from the United States, important contacts with American centres were developing. In 1819, after a locust plague, an expedition was sent from the Settlement to the Mississippi River to obtain seed grain. This was the beginning of a commercial connection between the Settlement and the United States that continued to grow. During the 1820s droves of cattle and sheep were brought in from as far away as Wisconsin, Missouri, and Kentucky. Simpson was not pleased with this development. His displeasure increased as, every summer, the trails echoed to the sound of hundreds of noisy Red River carts squeaking their way southward with furs. (On the return trip they carried manufactured goods, ironware, tea, and tobacco.) Trading in furs was illegal, but when the Hudson's Bay Company tried to prevent the export of furs from its territories, there were bitter complaints from both the free traders and the Métis, who had formed an alliance with the free traders against the Company. Increased trade with the United States provided employment for the Métis as tripmen conducting the carts across the prairie trails, first to St Paul and later to the post established by the Americans at Pembina. To prohibit their trading in furs, the Métis claimed, was contrary to their rights as natives of the soil.

They had other grievances. Although they formed a large part of the population of the Red River Settlement, the Métis had never been fairly represented on the Council of Assiniboia, the body appointed by the Hudson's Bay Company to govern the District of Assiniboia. And the Métis resented the

fact that the courts had never had competent French interpreters or a judge who would speak French.

These grievances, and the demand for free trade in furs,
came to a head in 1849 when William Sayer, a Métis, was
brought to trial charged with illegally trading in furs. Under
the guidance of James Sinclair, an English halfbreed, and
Father George Belcourt, the Métis were urged to demand
their rights as a separate and distinct community of people.
Another leader in this free-trade movement was Louis Riel's
father. On the day of the Sayer trial he urged the Métis to go
to the court house "armed and fully prepared to assert their
rights". The Métis did. About 400 armed men gathered near
the court house at Fort Garry. Sayer was found guilty—but
he was not sentenced. To the free traders and the Métis this
was a great victory. "Le commerce est libre!" the Métis
shouted. "Vive la liberté!" And it *was* a victory. Thereafter
the Hudson's Bay Company never attempted to enforce its
monoply in the courts.

Encouraged by the success of their agitation, the Métis
turned their attention to the judge, Adam Thom, whose
anti-French sentiments, they said, were an insult to their
"nation". They succeeded in forcing Thom's retirement from
the court. After 1850 they gained further satisfaction when
several Métis were appointed to the Council of Assiniboia—
though they never achieved what they really wanted: elected
representatives, members "chosen from our nation by our-
selves".

Louis Riel was five years old at the time of the Sayer
affair. All through his boyhood he absorbed a strong feeling
of nationality from stories of Métis hunting exploits, of Métis
victories over the Indians and over Semple at Seven Oaks, and

he acquired a sense of pride from them. His father—better educated than his fellow Métis, signer of petitions, orator in defence of Métis rights, activist in the Sayer affair—had a place in the community that brought him respect and that further identified young Louis with the Métis cause. As an adult he wrote that his father always "acted with wisdom" and would be "glorified". Louis would always speak of him with respect and reverence. He was closest, however, to his mother, who had almost become a nun before she married and whose strong piety greatly influenced him. "Family prayers, the rosary," he later wrote, "were always in my eyes and ears. And they are as much a part of my nature as the air I breathe. The calm reflective features of my mother, her eyes constantly turned towards heaven, her respect, her attention, her devotion to her religious obligations always left upon me the deepest impression of her good example." In 1870 his mother said of her eldest son: "He is everything to me, he is my life."

When Louis was seven he was sent to the Grey Sisters, who ran a girls' school in St Boniface to which young boys were admitted. There was no boys' school and Bishop Taché deplored the fact that Métis boys were not being educated. ("The Métis do not like to be governed by women," he wrote, "and this probably explains why their children do not go to school.") He persuaded some Christian Brothers to come from Canada* as teachers. When they started a boys' school in the Bishop's house, Louis left the Grey Sisters to receive his schooling there, in a room so small that the few students were crowded and the teacher could not sit down.

Louis did well at his studies. The Bishop kept a close

---

* Between 1841 and 1867, the year of Confederation, "Canada" refers to the Union of Canada, comprising present-day Ontario and Quebec.

watch on the schoolroom, always looking out for future priests, and he noticed Louis' progress. He arranged with some colleges in Quebec to take any students he found promising and in 1858 chose four Métis to go to Canada for further education: Louis Riel, Louis Schmidt, Daniel McDougall, and Joseph Nolin. On June 1 three of the four boys* received the Bishop's blessing and said goodbye to their families—in Riel's case his mother and his sister Sara: his father was away getting machinery for a mill. The parting was both sad and exciting. The Riels were a close family and Louis would be away from them for years. He was breaking his ties with everything that was familiar to him and was no doubt fearful of the unknown. But, being young, he thought less of this than of the fifteen-hundred-mile journey that lay ahead of him. To a thirteen-year-old this was an adventure.

On the first part of his journey to Montreal, Louis travelled by ox-cart through plains country familiar to all Métis. The boys were accompanied by Métis tripmen guiding a brigade of Red River carts to St Paul and by Sister Valade of the Grey Sisters who intended to recruit some nuns in Montreal. In the northwestern part of Minnesota, where the cart brigade crossed the Red Lake River, Louis had a joyful meeting with his father, who was returning from Montreal with his machinery. "The encounter of father and son was very touching," Louis Schmidt wrote later. Before young Louis returned to Red River, his father would be dead.

Twenty-eight days after starting, they arrived at St Paul and had their first really exciting experience when they sailed in a steamboat down the Mississippi to Prairie du Chien. Here another novelty awaited them: a train trip. They travelled by train to Chicago, then went on to Detroit and into Canada.

* The parents of Joseph Nolin would not let him go.

At Hamilton they ate their first oranges; in Toronto they spent a night in a convent; and on July 5, five weeks after starting out, they arrived in Montreal.

Louis was assigned to the College of Montreal, founded a hundred years before by the Sulpician Fathers. In September he became a boarder in an old building on St Paul and McGill Streets, where he began an enclosed life ruled by strict discipline and spartan routine.

An education at the College of Montreal, like that of any other classical college, lasted for eight years. Latin, Greek, French, and English were studied, along with some science and philosophy. Louis was a good student; his reports soon attested to this, with their highly favourable comments—a tribute to the schooling he had received at St Boniface. One of his fellow students, Eustache Prudhomme, wrote in 1870 that Louis was admired and respected by his classmates, that he was a charming young man who spoke with great fluency and was one of the best students. His teachers and friends noticed other traits, however. He was quick-tempered, moody, and argumentative, and he was very proud. "To offer an opinion contrary to his was to irritate him. He did not understand that everyone could not share his views, so much did he believe in his personal infallibility"—thus wrote another classmate, J. O. Mousseau. Louis usually spent his school holidays with Louis Schmidt. Once they ran the rapids of the St Lawrence at Sault St Louis, near Montreal. Sometimes they went to the home of the Tachés at Boucherville, sometimes to the Grey Sisters at Châteauguay.

In February 1864 Louis was greatly upset by the death of his father. His uncle, John Lee,* tried to console him and

---

* Lee was married to Lucie, the sister of Riel's father. A French Canadian of Irish origin, John Lee lived in Montreal.

discovered that Louis's mind seemed to be unhinged by grief. For a while his piety became exaggerated and eccentric and expressed itself in religious ravings; then he settled into a period of deep and silent melancholy. At school Louis was lonely and withdrawn and so restless and unsettled that his teachers were convinced he would never be a good priest. Louis himself was coming to the same conclusion and began to consider a career in business or the law. In March 1865 he came to a decision and left the college without taking a degree.

Having put aside his theological training, Louis found employment in the law office of Rodolphe LaFlamme, a French-Canadian nationalist and opponent of Confederation. The project for a union of the British North American provinces was at this time the main topic of political discussion. George Etienne Cartier, the leading French-Canadian supporter of the Confederation movement, was satisfied that French-Canadian rights and identity would be secure in the proposed union. Others, like LaFlamme and young Wilfrid Laurier, were of the opposite opinion. Laurier, just beginning his career as a lawyer and newspaper editor, wrote in 1866 that Confederation would be the "tomb" of French Canada. It would, he said, "kill French nationality" and French and Catholic elements "would be swallowed up" by the English and Protestant majority.

In LaFlamme's office Louis could not escape what was to him the new experience of political debate. He was excited by the intensity of the arguments of the young men of French Canada and stirred by their passionate approach to politics and ideas. His study of law became a secondary interest. More important to his later life was the expression of French-Canadian nationalism to which he was exposed at

Young Riel, about 1858

this time. It revived, perhaps, the memory of his father and the struggle of the Métis for recognition of the French language and for political representation in determining the affairs of the Red River Settlement.

After a year in LaFlamme's office, Louis—still restless and impatient, still searching for a career—made up his mind to return to Red River. This decision was hastened by his disappointment in a love affair. He had fallen in love with Marie Julie Guernon, the daughter of neighbours of his aunt and uncle, the Lees, with whom he was living. When her parents objected to their daughter's marrying a Métis, the engagement was broken off.

Little is known of Louis's life between this unhappy experience and his return home in the summer of 1868. For nearly two years he lived in Chicago, then in St Paul where, it is said, he worked in a dry-goods store. In St Paul he might have met some of the Red River Métis on their frequent trips to the city and heard from them disturbing news of affairs in the Settlement.

He arrived at St Boniface on July 28. "It was early in the morning when I saw my birthplace again," he wrote; "a Sunday, before sunrise. . . . I saw my very dear mother, brothers, and sisters that very same day."

2

Resistance

Riel was twenty-four years old when he went back to Red River. His mother and Bishop Taché were disappointed that he did not return as a priest; had he completed his training at the seminary in Montreal, he would have been the first of his people to enter the Church. After ten years in Montreal he was not trained for any particular work. About all that could be said of him was that he had received an education beyond that of any of the young Métis in the Settlement. And from other young men in the city he had learned about the political issues of the day.

Soon after his return, Riel invited his old school friend Louis Schmidt, who had returned to Red River in 1861, to live with him and his mother. Schmidt told him of many changes in the Settlement. Some of these Riel could see for himself. The cathedral of St Boniface, where he had attended his first mass, was gone; it had been destroyed by fire in 1860. In the place of the twin-turreted church he remembered was a single-spired building on the same site. Beside it was Bishop Taché's new stone house. Across the river at the forks of the Red and Assiniboine, Fort Garry still stood; the Hudson's Bay Company had enlarged it while Riel had been away, but it was still much the same. The high limestone walls with bastions at the corners made it look like a military

23

fort. No one had ever attacked it, however. In fact there were no troops or even well-trained men in the Settlement to defend it.

Fort Garry was a busier place now. After a steamboat was placed on the Red River in 1859 and St Paul, Minnesota, was connected by railway with the East in 1862, the Hudson's Bay Company found it cheaper to bring goods into its territories from the south rather than through Hudson Bay. York Factory on the Bay, which had been the Company's most important depot, began to decline in importance and its place in outfitting the fur brigades and distributing trade goods throughout the Northwest was gradually taken over by Fort Garry. There was a constant coming and going of boats and carts at the Fort—heavily laden York boats heading for Lake Winnipeg and the Saskatchewan posts and ox-driven Red River carts lumbering back and forth between Fort Garry and St Paul.

Riel saw a great many of these noisy big-wheeled vehicles in and around the Settlement. American steamboats on the Red—first the box-like *Anson Northup,* then the *International*—did not bring an end to them. In 1869, 2,500 Red River carts were employed in transporting furs and goods between St Paul and Fort Garry. At this time there was little commercial connection between the Northwest and Canada, and many people in the Red River Settlement were convinced that the Northwest would one day become part of the United States. The Americans in St Paul, and some of them in the Settlement, were working to bring this about. They wanted to get a railway built from St Paul to Fort Garry. They believed that if the Northwest could be bound more closely to the United States by trade and transportation, it would soon be forced to join politically with the American union.

Winnipeg, 1869. Dr. Schultz's store is the building with the flag, on which the word "Canada" appears

Perhaps the biggest change that had taken place during Riel's absence could be observed about a mile north of Fort Garry. There, at the edge of the Hudson's Bay Company reserve, a little village called Winnipeg had developed where Louis as a boy had known only a couple of stores owned by Andrew McDermot and his son-in-law A. G. B. Bannatyne. Now other merchants had put up buildings and houses. There was a mill, a butcher shop, a gun shop, a harness store, a drug store, a bookshop, a photographer's store, a newspaper office, two churches, two saloons, and a hotel. Just beyond the village were the river lots of the Selkirk settlers, and further down the Red River was St Andrew's, a settlement of retired fur traders and English halfbreed families. Along the Assiniboine, fifty miles to the west, was a new settlement of Canadians—that is, people from Ontario—called Portage la Prairie.

Riel heard criticism of the Canadians who were living in the village of Winnipeg. They had become very unpopular with the Métis. Some of these newcomers boastfully spoke of taking over the government from the Hudson's Bay Company and making many changes in the Settlement. They were opposed to the Hudson's Bay Company government, they even made fun of it. They wanted to see the Northwest become part of Canada. Their newspaper, the *Nor'Wester,* the only one in the Settlement, kept repeating that the people at Red River wanted to be annexed to Canada. This was not true, Riel learned. The *Nor'Wester* was aware that it did not represent all the people, but it had little respect for the opinions of others, calling its opponents "sneaking, cowardly, mean, and contemptible".

The newspaper spoke for only one active group in the Settlement—the Canadians. Others, like the Selkirk settlers and the English halfbreeds, seemed to be satisfied under the government of the Hudson's Bay Company, yet these people were not disturbed by the possibility of annexation to Canada. As for the Métis, they feared the end of Company rule and annexation to Canada and thought this would mean a rush of settlers into the country from Ontario—English-speaking Protestants opposed to the French language and the Roman Catholic Church. What would happen to the Métis if these newcomers were like the Canadians of the *Nor'Wester*? Had not the newspaper referred to the Métis offensively when it said that the "indolent and careless" of the country must "fall back before the march of a superior intelligence"? Riel could see that the Métis were frightened and he recognized in their complaints and criticisms the same fears the young men in Montreal had expressed about Confederation. The Métis too were worried about their language and their religion.

Everyone in the Settlement was talking about the pending sale of the Hudson's Bay Company territories to Canada. The Company, Canada, and the British government had been carrying on negotiations for years, but the people at Red River had never been consulted. Not even the Hudson's Bay Company officers at Fort Garry were kept informed about what decisions were reached. To the Company in London, and the governments of Britain and Canada, the transfer was a legal and financial act to be performed in London. No consideration was given to what the people at Red River might think.

The autumn of 1867 and the spring of 1868 were a time of economic distress at Red River. Not only was there little rain and therefore poor crops, but what did grow was soon devoured by a plague of grasshoppers. Father Jean-Marie

Lestanc of St Boniface wrote that the voracious insects were everywhere—like "snow in the air and as flakes of snow on the ground. They penetrated into the parlours and kitchens, bed chambers and bedding, pots, pans, kettles, ovens, boots and coat pockets. One scarcely dared to open one's mouth." The Settlement was close to starvation. "Within the colony not one bushel will be harvested," said Bishop Taché. "Moreover," he added, "the buffalo hunters, instead of furnishing their large hunting share of provisions, arrived starving from their usual hunting grounds." Even rabbits and fish were scarce in those years. To help the needy families, money was sent from England, Canada, and the United States.

In the summer of 1868, without seeking permission of the Hudson's Bay Company, the Canadian government sent road builders into the country as part of a relief program; the project was intended to provide employment for the men in the Settlement and to bring money into the country with which the people could buy food and seed grain. The road was to run from Fort Garry to Lake of the Woods as part of a road-and-water system connecting the Red River Settlement with Canada. Like the Americans in St Paul, the Canadians in Ontario wanted to establish a closer and easier connection with the Northwest. But the men sent to supervise the project were not good ambassadors of Canada. They were a boisterous, unruly group and looked down on the halfbreed people. "They behaved very badly," wrote Riel; "they nearly murdered each other on certain occasions" and "did not impress the inhabitants of the country very favourably." He was referring to an incident when the workers argued with the superintendent of the road project, John A. Snow, about their pay. When he refused to increase their wages they threatened to drown him. The ringleader in this affair was a hot-headed Irish-Canadian of about twenty-eight by the name of Thomas Scott. He and the others were brought to trial and fined £4 for assault, after which Scott said it was too bad they had not thrown Snow into the river when they were at it and got their money's worth.

What aroused the Métis most against these Canadians was the fear that their lands would be taken away from them. Many of the Métis were only squatters. They had no legal title to their property, and as land had passed from father to son or been sold to someone else in the Settlement, the transactions had never been recorded. They became alarmed when they found that men on the road project and other Canadians in the Settlement were starting to buy land cheaply from the Indians—land that the Métis thought was theirs.

One of these Canadians found out how dangerous it was to insult the halfbreed people. Charles Mair was a poet from Ontario who had come to Red River as paymaster on the government road project. He wrote a number of letters to his brother in Perth describing his journey to the Northwest and the magnificent tracts of fertile land available for settlers. In these letters Mair also made some unflattering remarks about the halfbreeds, particularly the halfbreed women. Unfortunately his brother forwarded these letters to a newspaper, which printed them. When the newspaper reached the Red River Settlement the insulted ladies were indignant. One day, when Mair appeared in the post office in Winnipeg, they attacked him. One lady pulled his nose, another his ears. Finally Mrs A. G. B. Bannatyne, the wife of the merchant, drove him from the building with a horsewhip.

Riel too was indignant at what Mair had written. In a letter he sent to a Quebec newspaper he charged Mair with spreading falsehoods about Red River and suggested that the poet

Thomas Scott, about 1863

should concentrate on writing verse, "for in that way his writings would make up in rhyme what they lack in reason."

Mair, like the other Canadians on the road project, made the mistake of associating too closely with the unpopular Canadians who were already living in the Settlement—men like J. C. Schultz, a doctor and trader and a fellow Ontarian who had been demanding changes for many years and who happened to be an agent for the road builders. Invited to move from "Dutch" George's hotel* in Winnipeg to Schultz's house, Mair was very glad to escape "the racket of a motley crowd of halfbreeds, playing billiards and drinking, to the quiet and solid comfort of a home."

To the Métis the road builders were a symbol of everything they feared if the Northwest became part of Canada. The Canadians threatened their existence as a distinct people, their language, their religion, and their lands. It did no good to remind them that the language and religious rights of French Canadians in Quebec had been preserved in the Confederation of 1867. Riel had been in Montreal when the negotiations that led to Confederation had taken place and was well aware that the French-Canadian leaders had taken part. Then should not the people of Red River be consulted if there was to be a change in the government of the Northwest? Should not someone make certain that consideration would be given to protecting the rights of the Métis? Who at Red River would speak up for the Métis?

Canada was not ready to listen to anyone about the fears and growing resentment at Red River. Robert Machray, the Anglican bishop of Rupert's Land, warned the Canadian government that trouble was developing. William Mactavish, a chief factor of the Hudson's Bay Company and governor of

* Owned by George Emmerling.

Rupert's Land, said to Bishop Taché in 1869: "I have just returned from Ottawa, and although I have been for forty years in the country, and Governor for fifteen years, I have not been able to cause any of my recommendations to be accepted by the Government. Those gentlemen are of opinion that they know a great deal more about this country than we do." He was ignored and Taché received the same treatment when he warned George Etienne Cartier, a cabinet minister, about unrest in the Settlement. Cartier was not interested in hearing what Taché had to say. "He knew it all a great deal better than I did," said Taché, " and did not want any information."

Riel was troubled, but like the other Métis he did not know what to do. Some of them began to keep a close watch on the movements of Canadians in the Settlement. When Mair and Snow appeared at St Norbert to examine the land and pace out lots, they were told to leave. A patrol was organized to warn any other strangers found in the Métis parishes to stay away from Métis lands. In July 1869 a group of halfbreeds, French- and English-speaking, met at the little court house just outside the gates of Fort Garry. Some demanded that the money to be paid by Canada to the Hudson's Bay Company for its territories be turned over to the Indians and halfbreeds. One man suggested that they seize the Company's property at Red River. Riel, who was present at this meeting, disapproved of such a move and spoke against it. The meeting broke up without any agreement on the steps to be taken. A few months later, however, a crisis occurred that demanded action.

In the fall of 1869, before the formal transfer of the country to Canada took place, the Canadian government sent a party of surveyors under J. S. Dennis to the Red River

Settlement. Canada this time sought permission of the Hud
son's Bay Company, and Dennis had been instructed not to
disturb existing property arrangements. Even with such pre
cautions Governor Mactavish, who understood well the mood
of the Métis people, thought the surveys were a dangerous
step. He was certain the Métis would try to stop the survey
ors from carrying out their work.

Standing in front of St Boniface Cathedral, Riel now spoke
out publicly—the first of many times he was to use his
powers of oratory to sway a Métis audience.* He charged
that the surveys were a threat to Métis lands. Dennis wrote to
Ottawa saying that the Métis might become violent. The
government told him to go ahead with the work and Dennis
did so, but cautiously. He avoided Métis property along the
river and began at the American border to run a survey line
back of this property to the north, from which individual lots
could later be marked out.

A Red River farm lot ran two miles back from the river.
Beyond the two miles the owner, by custom, had the use of a
further two miles for grazing his cattle or sheep; this outer
two miles was his hay privilege. In October 1869 Dennis's
men were working just south of Fort Garry, running their
survey line on the "hay privilege" of André Nault, Riel's
cousin. Nault protested to the surveyors but they did not
understand French. He then went for help. About eighteen
unarmed neighbours, led by Riel, returned to Nault's farm,

* In 1912 his friend Louis Schmidt wrote: "Riel was a born orator. . . . By nature
enthusiastic and a little exalted, his speeches made a great impression on crowds.
And then, the cause he had to defend—a cause noble and just to a rare degree—
was already in itself a natural stimulus to enthusiasm. Thus it is not astonishing to
see the effect that he had on simple and honest natures, such as were those of the
Métis, when he revealed to them their most sacred rights trampled under foot in
the invasion of their country by Canada."

tood on the surveyors' chain, and told them to stop. When
Mactavish later asked why he had done this, Riel answered
that the Canadian government had no right to make surveys
until the transfer had been completed and without the permission of the people of the Settlement.

The stopping of the surveys was the first act of resistance to
Canada's acquisition of the Northwest. It also revealed to the
Métis people that in Louis Riel they had found a champion—
someone who would speak for them and was prepared to
defend their rights and ensure their survival.

Just previous to this incident a number of Métis had begun
to hold meetings at St Norbert and St Vital to decide what
they should do about William McDougall, who had been
appointed by the Canadian government as Lieutenant-Governor of the Northwest and was on his way through the United
States to the Settlement to assume office. Out of these
meetings developed the National Committee of the Métis.
When the Committee heard that McDougall was bringing
cases of rifles and ammunition, they resolved that he should
not be allowed to come into the country. On October 21,
1869 they built a barricade on the road south of Fort Garry
and sent a communication to McDougall, who was then
approaching Pembina on the American side of the border. It
read: "The National Committee of the Métis of Red River
orders William McDougall not to enter the Territory of the
North West without special permission of the above-men-
tioned committee." It was signed "Louis Riel, Secretary".
This was the second act of resistance to Canada.

Once again Riel was asked to explain his actions. He was
summoned to meet with the Council of Assiniboia, the body
appointed by the Hudson's Bay Company to govern the Red
River Settlement and surrounding area and still the legal

government of the country. The Council called the Métis
actions "outrageous". Riel replied that the Métis people were
perfectly satisfied with the government of the Hudson's Bay
Company and wanted no other. They objected to the imposi-
tion of any new government without their consent and they
"would never admit any Governor no matter by whom he
might be appointed" unless delegates were sent first with
whom they might negotiate the terms and conditions of a
new government. In the same speech Riel explained further
why the Métis were resisting the transfer of the country to
Canada before the people were consulted. The Métis people,
Riel said, were "uneducated and only half civilized and felt
that if a large immigration were to take place they would
probably be crowded out of a country which they claimed as
their own." They thought they were acting for the good of
the whole Settlement. They did not think they were breaking
the law but acting "in defence of their liberty", and hoped
the English-speaking people in the Settlement would join
them in securing their "common rights".

The members of the Council tried to convince Riel that
Métis rights were not in danger. They pointed out that the
actions taken were "criminal" and might have "disastrous
consequences". And they advised Riel to use his influence
with the Métis to allow McDougall to come in.

The Council might argue with Riel but they could not
change his views. He refused to accept the Council's advice
and expressed his determination to oppose McDougall's
entry. He was firm, even stubborn, in his opinions and could
not be swayed. He had a small force of men, the only armed
force in the Settlement. The Council knew this and realized it
had no men or police with which to oppose him. There was
the danger that if it attempted to raise a force, a civil war

might result. So the Council of Assiniboia, the government of the country, was powerless. It disapproved of Riel's actions, but all it could do in response to his ultimatum to McDougall was to send a messenger to McDougall advising him to remain at the border outside the Hudson's Bay Company territories.

Riel never thought of himself as a rebel. He had declared that the Métis were loyal subjects of the Queen. Yet each step he took led directly to the formation of a government to replace that of the Council of Assiniboia. Early in November 1869 Riel, with some of his men, headed for Fort Garry, and they were followed by others—about 120 in all. They walked quietly through the unguarded gates of the Hudson's Bay Company Fort and took possession. When they were challenged by a chief factor, Dr Cowan, Riel said he was there to protect the Fort from a danger—by which he meant, to prevent the Canadians from doing the same thing. The Hudson's Bay Company, like the Council of Assiniboia, had no armed force and could do nothing to challenge him.

Riel then attempted to gain the co-operation of other groups in the Settlement. A few days after seizing Fort Garry, he issued an invitation to the English-speaking parishes to send delegates to meet the representatives of the French at the court house; the political state of the Settlement would be considered and measures for its welfare adopted. The meetings of this convention revealed a pronounced and serious difference of opinion between the English and French parts of the community. The English disapproved of Riel's treatment of McDougall and the occupation of Fort Garry. A proclamation from Governor Mactavish was read out. It protested against "unlawful acts and intents" and beseeched those involved to disperse. It concluded: "You are dealing with a crisis out of which may come incalculable good or immeasurable evil . . . let me finally charge you to adopt such means as are lawful and constitutional, rational and safe.' When James Ross, a Scottish halfbreed and a former editor of the *Nor'Wester*, stated that the Métis had started a rebellion Riel spoke out angrily. As he himself later recounted in his notes, he said:

"If we rebel against the Company which sold us and against Canada which wishes to buy us, we do not rebel against the English government, which has not yet given its approval to the actual transfer of the country. What! We recognize the government of Assiniboia so far as it exists.' (*Laughter.*)

Ross. "You make a pretence of recognizing it."

Riel, turning to the French. "Do we indeed only pretend to recognize it? Come, speak." (*All:* "No! No!") "Moreover, we are faithful to our native land. We shall protect it against the dangers which menace it. We wish that the people of Red River be a free people. Let us help one another. We are all brothers and kindred, says Mr Ross, and it is true. Let us not separate. See what Mr Mactavish [says]. He says that from this assembly and from the decisions of this assembly can come an inestimable good. Let us unite. The evil that is feared will not take place."

At one of the meetings towards the end of November, Riel startled the English representatives by suggesting the formation of a Provisional Government to replace the Council of Assiniboia. The English did not like this proposal: it seemed like a further act of rebellion. The English and French did agree, however, on a List of Rights that Riel proposed at the convention. The list included the demand for an elected legislature, representation in the Canadian Parliament, recognition of both the French and English languages, and the confirmation of existing customs and usages at Red River. Despite this agreement the convention broke up on the question of what to do about McDougall. The English thought McDougall should be allowed to enter the country and that their grievances should be placed before him. Riel insisted that McDougall should not be allowed in until he guaranteed that the demands in the List of Rights would be granted.

While these meetings were going on, the Canadians in the settlement had kept in touch with McDougall at Pembina. McDougall—described by Alexander Begg* as having "an overbearing, distant, and unpleasant manner"—hoped through the Canadians to undermine Riel's leadership and his control of the Settlement. The Queen's Proclamation declaring the country to be part of Canada was to take effect on December 1, 1869, and McDougall expected to become Governor of the Northwest. On that day he took it upon himself to step across the border and read a Proclamation announcing the transfer. Then, because of the bitter cold and to avoid the Métis patrol, he hurried back to Pembina. He did not know that the Canadian government, on hearing of Riel's activities, had postponed the transfer: McDougall was still not legally Governor of the country. Nevertheless he appointed J. S. Dennis as "Conservator of the Peace" and authorized him to raise and equip a force of men to arrest and disarm the Métis, who were said to be "unlawfully assembled" at Red River. Dr Schultz, eager to advance the transfer of the country to Canada, wanted to attack Fort Garry at once, but Dennis, who was always over-cautious, hesitated: he did not want to make any move until he had gathered enough men. As it turned out, he was never able to raise a force sufficient to

Begg was a trading partner of A. G. B. Bannatyne and lived in Winnipeg.

challenge Riel. Even though many were opposed to Riel, they did not wish to take part in what might have been a civil war in the Settlement.

Riel, expecting to be attacked by the Canadians, moved first. On December 7, 1869 he and his men left Fort Garry and surrounded Dr Schultz's store. They demanded the surrender of Schultz and forty-eight armed Canadians assembled there and marched them to Fort Garry as prisoners. The next day Riel issued a "Declaration of the People" announcing the establishment of a Provisional Government and offering to enter into negotiations with the Canadian government about the terms on which Red River would enter Confederation. On December 10 a white flag with a fleur-de-lys was raised on the flagpole in the square at Fort Garry—the flag of the Provisional Government. Riel became President of this government and his friend Louis Schmidt Secretary.

McDougall found himself in a humiliating position. The Canadian government that had appointed him now criticized him for his premature move in declaring Canadian sovereignty in the Northwest. McDougall had been prevented from entering the country he had expected to govern; there was nothing for him to do but leave Pembina and return to Canada. The Americans, who were watching developments both at Pembina and St Paul, were amused at his predicament and referred to him as "a King without a Kingdom".

The Canadian government was aware that Americans in St Paul hoped the difficulties at Red River would lead to annexation of the country to the United States. The Prime Minister, Sir John A. Macdonald, saw the acquisition of Red River as a vital part of his policy of developing a Canada that would stretch across the prairies to the Pacific Ocean. He was determined that the Americans should not thwart his plan.

Riel's resistance to Canadian rule forced Macdonald to take the kind of action that should have been taken years before. He decided to send a "Special Commissioner" to Fort Garry to explain to the people the principles on which Canada intended to govern the country, and to make a report on the causes of the disturbances. The man chosen to undertake this mission was Donald A. Smith, the head of the Hudson's Bay Company in Canada. Although Smith had been with the Company since 1838, he had never served in the West. Much of his life had been spent in Labrador. He had come to Canada when he was eighteen and his first job with the Company had been counting muskrat skins at its Lachine establishment. Many years later he would become the chief shareholder and, as Lord Strathcona, Governor of the Company.

Smith arrived at Fort Garry on December 27, 1869 and went to see Riel immediately. Riel was cautious, suspecting that Smith had come to undermine his authority at Red River. He was conscious that his position was not a secure one. Even though he was President of the Provisional Government and had at his command the only armed force in the Settlement, he was troubled because he had not been able to secure the co-operation of the English-speaking parts of the Settlement. He and his men watched Smith's movements carefully.

After several interviews with Riel, Smith suggested a mass meeting at which he could explain Canada's policy. Two meetings were arranged, for January 19 and 20, 1870. Though it was twenty degrees below zero, a thousand people gathered for the first meeting inside the walls of Fort Garry. The speakers they had come to hear, Smith and Riel, appeared in front of a large house—the residence of the Company's officers and clerks—on a gallery that had an outdoor stairway leading up to it. Smith made a speech and then read government documents he had brought with him. Riel acted as interpreter. Stamping their feet and swinging their arms in the cold, the people listened restlessly for five hours.

With little difficulty Smith won their confidence. He assured them that Canada did not intend to interfere with their property, language or religion. Riel seemed satisfied, even though Smith had no authority to make any guarantee on behalf of the government of Canada.

At the end of the second day Riel admitted he had come to the meeting "with fear". "We are not yet enemies," he said to his audience, "but we came very near being so. As soon as we understood each other, we joined in demanding what our English fellow-subjects in common with us believe to be our just rights. I am not afraid to say 'our rights' for we all have rights. We claim no half-rights, mind you, but all the rights we are entitled to. Those rights will be set forth by our representatives, and what is more, gentlemen, we will get them." Several times during this speech the crowd interrupted with loud cheers and the meeting broke up with the feeling that the crisis at Red River was over.

In his last speech Riel had suggested that French and English representatives give consideration to Smith's mission. The spirit of goodwill that had flowed through the meeting with Smith did not carry over into the representatives' meetings, however. While the representatives were discussing a new Bill of Rights, it became clear that Riel could no longer have his own way unopposed. He never accepted criticism or opposition easily and when he found that some of the Métis representatives were not prepared to accept several of his suggestions, he gave vent to uncontrolled outbursts of temper.

Smith had been invited to attend these meetings. As each item of the Bill of Rights was discussed, Riel asked him if he could guarantee that the Canadian government would agree. Smith could not do so. He had no authority to accept the Bill of Rights on behalf of the Canadian government but suggested that delegates be sent to Ottawa to discuss it with the government. This satisfied Riel and the representatives, who then organized at Riel's demand a new Provisional Government—the English parts of the Settlement had never accepted the earlier government proclaimed by Riel in December 1869. Riel felt that he had at last achieved one of his goals. His aim had been to unite all parts of the Settlement and then proceed to negotiate with Canada. "United," he said to the representatives, "we command a hearing from Canada, where our rights are to come from, which we can command in no other way. It is also to be borne in mind that a feeling of insecurity reigns in the minds of the people which can be successfully combatted in no other way than by a union."

Many of the representatives were hesitant, not sure that a Provisional Government would be legal, but they agreed to Riel's demand for one. Some of them felt they had no choice; they were convinced that if they did not agree, Riel would act alone. This second Provisional Government was established on February 10 and the delegates appointed to go to Ottawa were Father N. J. Ritchot, Riel's strongest supporter among the clergy; Judge John Black, a former Hudson's Bay Company employee; and A. H. Scott, an American bartender living in the Red River Settlement.

Of the prisoners Riel had taken to Fort Garry in December, some had been given their freedom early in January on condition they leave the country or take an oath of allegience to the Provisional Government and not take up arms against

it; several—including Dr Schultz, Charles Mair, and Thomas Scott—had escaped. At the mass meetings Smith addressed and at the meeting of representatives that organized the new Provisional Government, the question of the remaining prisoners was brought up. Riel agreed to release them once the new government had been established, and by the middle of February they had been freed.

In the meantime trouble was brewing at Portage la Prairie, where a group of settlers from Canada—led without much conviction by Major C. A. Boulton, a surveyor, and including the escapees, Charles Mair and the volatile Orangeman, Thomas Scott—were making plans to storm Fort Garry, release Riel's prisoners, and overthrow the Provisional Government. The group was badly organized and poorly armed, however, and completely incapable of carrying out such a move against Riel's Métis forces. Moreover, it had little support in the Settlement; most of the settlers disapproved of aggressive action and saw only the possibility of a civil war between the Métis and the Canadians. Nevertheless Boulton and his men began their march on February 12 to Kildonan Presbyterian Church, a few miles north of the Fort. There Schultz joined them with supporters from lower down the Red River.

On February 15 a young Métis named Norbert Parisien was brought to the church as a suspected spy and spent the night imprisoned beneath the pulpit. The next morning he was permitted to go outside with a guard and two men. Catching sight of a gun lying on the seat of a cutter, he bolted from the guard, seized the gun, and dashed for the river. It happened that young Hugh Sutherland was riding across the frozen river, and Parisien, thinking that Sutherland was after him, shot him. Parisien was fired at, captured, and treated roughly. The next day he was shot when he tried to escape again. Sutherland died within twenty-four hours, Parisien on March 4.

This occurrence frightened the Canadians, and when they heard that Riel had released the prisoners, Schultz's party lost heart for the attack on the Fort and began to disperse. The men from Portage la Prairie also decided to head for home. As the road would have taken them near Fort Garry they decided to cross the open prairie despite the deep snow because this route would keep them distant from the Fort. Major Boulton tells us in his *Reminiscences of the North-West Rebellions* (1886) that they were "anxious to avoid a conflict and to return to our homes peaceably".

At last we started out across the plains in single file, following closely in one another's footsteps on account of the depth of the snow, which was up to our waists; and in this order we marched until we got opposite the Fort, when we observed a party of men on horseback issuing out of it. They marched towards us, followed about two hundred yards in the rear by some fifty men on foot. We kept steadily on our way, without hesitation, until they approached within a hundred and fifty yards, when some of the men asked for orders, whether we should form up for defence. I gave strict orders that on no account should a shot be fired or any hostility be provoked; and the party on horseback, numbering about fifty, continued to approach us. . . . The party, headed by O'Donoghue and Lépine, then came forward, and O'Donoghue asked: "What party is this?" I answered: "It is a party of men returning to the Portage." He then asked: "Is Major Boulton here?" I replied that I was the man, at which he expressed pleasure and informed me that Riel had sent him out from the Fort to meet us and to invite us to the Fort to hold a parley. I told him that we wished to go on our way without interference.

While this conversation was going on, Lépine went up to one of the men, named Murdoch Macleod, a fine young Scotchman who belonged to my party. He had his revolver in his hand and Lépine attempted to wrest it from him. This was an aggressive movement on Lépine's part, and no doubt intended to provoke hostilities. I was afraid that in the struggle the revolver would go off, which would be the signal for a massacre from which there was no escape. We were not armed; we were up to our waists in snow; and in the presence of double our number, who were well armed, supported by a large force in the Fort near by and who were excited over the events of the previous day. Under the circumstances I knew that it would be criminal to jeopardize the lives of the settlers who formed the party, many of whom had left large families at home. I therefore ordered Macleod to give up the revolver and signalled the party to follow me to the Fort. . . .

We reached the Fort in about half an hour, and, entering the gates, which were at once closed behind us, we were immediately surrounded by about four hundred men.

Boulton's men were disarmed and imprisoned. Riel decided to take a hard stand with Boulton, who was put in a room by himself, handcuffed, and chained at the legs.

I was given an old buffalo robe to lie down on, and a pitcher of water and a piece of pemmican were placed by my side. Shortly after this I heard the door open and Riel looked in. Without entering, he said: "Major Boulton, you prepare to die tomorrow at twelve o'clock." I answered: "Very well," and he retired.

Though Boulton took this calmly, the news, when it reached the Settlement outside the walls of the Fort, caused widespread alarm. Several people—the parents of Hugh Sutherland included—pleaded with Riel to spare Boulton's life with no success. Donald Smith appeared before Riel and told him the execution would destroy the unity that made the Provisional Government possible—that civil war would result if it took place. When he said he would use his influence to bring over the English-speaking settlers to Riel's side and to get them to elect members to the council of the Provisional Government, Riel called off the execution. He could see that he had suddenly acquired a dominant position with the Canadian government's representative, having asserted his power by forcing Smith to assist his Provisional Government.

After a bout of illness—he had what was called "brain fever", which his mother nursed him through at the Fort—Riel turned his mind to the prisoners. The most unruly of them was Thomas Scott. He had attacked the guards, called the Métis a pack of cowards, insulted their religion, and threatened to assassinate Riel. The guards hated him and could easily have been on the point of killing him. On March 3 he was brought before a court martial and charged with insubordination—punished as a crime on the buffalo hunt—and with having taken up arms against the Provisional Government. The hastily organized court of Métis examined several witnesses, including Riel. When Scott was brought in, Riel had to read the charges, explain the evidence, and translate the court's decision, since no one spoke English as well as he did. A few days before, Scott had said: "I believe they are bad enough to shoot me, but I can hardly think that they dare do it." They dared: by a majority vote Scott was condemned to death.

At first Scott thought this sentence was meant to intimidate the Canadian prisoners, and so did the Rev. George Young, a Methodist minister. Young went to see the Métis chief. Riel told him that Scott was "a very bad man, and has insulted my guards and has hindered some from making peace; so I must make an example to impress others and lead them to respect my government, and will take him first, and then, if necessary, others will follow." Donald Smith was the next man to plead with Riel. To Smith's arguments Riel said: "We must make Canada respect us." He went on: "I have done three good things since I commenced. I have spared Boulton's life at your instance, and I do not regret it, for he is a fine fellow; I pardoned Gaddy,* and he showed his gratitude by escaping out of the bastion, but I do not grudge him his miserable life; and now I shall shoot Scott."

The execution took place the next morning. After saying "Goodbye, boys" to his fellow prisoners, Scott was taken with Young down an outside stairway of his quarters and through the gate of the Fort. "This is horrible!" he said to Young. "This is cold-blooded murder! Be sure to make a true statement!" Outside the walls of the Fort a white bandage was tied over his eyes, and then at noon, in front of a small crowd, with Riel hovering in the background, a firing squad raised its guns and fired at the kneeling Scott. He fell forward, struggling. The coup de grâce was delivered with a revolver shot.†

Why did Riel allow such an unnecessary and cruel sentence to be carried out? It was unlike him to use violence. He had

* William Gaddy, an English-speaking halfbreed scout who had been captured on February 14.

† George Young in his *Manitoba Memories* (1897) and Major Boulton in his *Reminiscences* give space to the story that Scott lived for some hours after he was shot. Young quotes the account in the St Paul *Press* of Henry Robinson, a former editor of the *New Nation,* who claimed to have been shown the coffin and to have heard anguished pleas for help issuing from it. Riel and a sentry are said to have put an end to his life *then.* Boulton quotes the account of John Bruce, a Métis who had fallen out with Riel. The two authors were given to believing and disseminating anything that put Riel in a bad light and the reports of Scott's lingering death are questionable.

simply wanted to unify the people of Red River, to establish a strong government that could negotiate with Canada the conditions of Canadian rule in the Settlement. In pursuing these aims he had tried to avoid bloodshed. But Riel was ambitious and proud, filled with a sense of mission and dedication to his people. And he not only resented opposition, he had a fiery temper.

Riel stated his reasons for allowing Scott to die. Scott, he said, had recruited about a hundred men and led a revolt against the Provisional Government. He was a violent prisoner. He incited other prisoners to attack the guards. To Riel, Scott had become a symbol of opposition. As President of the government Riel needed to assert his authority. He had to prove that his government could govern the community and maintain law and order. He particularly needed to impress on the Canadians in the Settlement that his government must be obeyed. "We wanted to be sure that our attitude was taken seriously," Riel wrote to a friend in Quebec. To Smith he had said: "We must make Canada respect us." This is why he was deaf to those, like Smith, who pleaded with him to spare Scott's life; why he did not simply expel Scott from the country; why he committed a blunder that would forever tarnish his career and label him in the eyes of the excitable anti-Catholic Orangemen of Ontario a murderer.

3

Member of Parliament

Spring was on its way and the fur trade would soon make its demands on Fort Garry. There had been no activity in the fur trade since Riel occupied the Fort. One result of this inactivity was that money was not being circulated. Riel knew the importance of the fur trade and offered to make a bargain with the Hudson's Bay Company. He agreed to release the Fort and its supplies, to permit the Company to reopen the trade, and he promised peace. In return he demanded recognition of the Provisional Government, a large loan, and £4,000 for provisions and the support of his military force. Governor Mactavish had to accept. "The Hudson's Bay Company can now resume business," said Riel's Proclamation of April 9. "Themselves contributing to the public good, they circulate their money as of old." As the Fort was still the "seat of Government", a guard of fifty men was retained and Riel continued to live there.

Things then settled down at Red River. The name of Thomas Scott was hardly mentioned. The most vocal Canadians—Schultz and Mair—were in Canada, the Portage men were imprisoned in the Fort, the community was peaceful, and Riel for the moment felt secure.

"Riel does not appear to be gaining in popularity," Alexander Begg wrote in his journal on April 18; "—his putting on so much style as he is now doing does not tend to increase him in favor even with his own people. He could not rule very long here." However, an American visitor was impressed by him. When the ex-governor of Minnesota, William R. Marshall, paid a visit to Red River late in April, one of his party* described the Métis leader:

Riel was about 28 years of age [he was 26], has a fine physique, of active temperament, a great worker, and I think is able to endure a great deal. He is a large man, with a high forehead (not broad), of very winning persuasive manners; and in his whole bearing, energy and ready decision are prominent characteristics; and in this fact lies his great powers, for I should not give him credit for great profundity, yet he is sagacious, and I think thoroughly patriotic and no less thoroughly incorruptible. In his intercourse with us he was very diplomatic and non-committal. Yet there was nothing offensive in this, but rather it appeared to me to be a merit in him.

On April 20 an incident occurred over the flag. Riel gave orders to have the "Union Jack" raised over the Fort and W. B. O'Donoghue, a supporter of Riel who was nevertheless in favour of American annexation, had it taken down. Alexander Begg reports that

. . . when Riel found out he came out and said that when he gave orders he wished them obeyed, and further that if O'Donoghue was working for selfish ends or Annexation to the States he might go where he could get them, and that he deserved to go to jail. If anyone wanted the Provisional flag hoisted it could be done so under the British one as under the protection of it. Riel then hoisted or rather ordered to be hoisted the Union Jack. O'Donoghue and some of his follow-

* N. P. Langford.

*ers threatened to leave on account of this but it appears
thought better of it.*

*Riel reminded O'Donoghue that he had sworn himself as a
British subject.*

Riel was worried about the delegates in Canada, from
whom he had not heard. They had left Red River for Ottawa
a few weeks after the shooting of Scott, travelling overland
by horse and sleigh, then stage-coach, to St Cloud, Minnesota. From there Father Ritchot and A. H. Scott took the
train to St Paul, Chicago, Buffalo, and Ogdensburg, New
York, where they were met by a Dominion policeman sent
by the Canadian government to provide protection on the
last part of the journey to Ottawa. Judge Black travelled to
Ottawa via Detroit and Toronto.

Sir John A. Macdonald had already made plans to send a
military expedition to Fort Garry. In the meantime he and
George Etienne Cartier, the senior French Canadian in the
cabinet, prepared to meet with the delegates to discuss the
Bill of Rights drawn up by the representatives at Red River
and then amended in several respects by Riel and his council.
The most important changes were that Assiniboia should
enter Confederation as a province called Manitoba, not as a
territory, and that both Protestant and Catholic schools
should receive public support as they did in the province of
Quebec.

Before the delegates arrived in Ottawa, racial and religious
passions in Ontario had been aroused against Riel. Public
meetings and demonstrations were organized in a number of
communities to hear Dr Schultz and Charles Mair. At a
Toronto meeting—which had to move from the St Lawrence
Hall to the front of the City Hall because of the crowd—

5,000 were present. It was one of the noisiest and most enthusiastic meetings the city had ever seen. When Dr Schultz stood up to speak, the crowd cheered. "We'll hang Riel!" they cried. Resolutions were passed demanding that the government refuse to meet with the delegates from the "rebel" government at Fort Garry. Newspapers throughout the province cried for revenge. "The rebellion must be put down," said the Toronto *Globe*. "Riel has taken the life of a Canadian"; he and his accomplices must be brought to trial. The execution of Thomas Scott was called a "barbarous murder" by an Ontario member of Parliament. Dr J. S. Lynch, a Canadian who had been in Red River, wrote to the Governor-General that Red River had been the scene of treason, robbery, and murder; Scott had been "butchered in cold blood". When Ritchot and A. H. Scott arrived in Ottawa, they were arrested, on a warrant sworn by Thomas Scott's brother, for aiding in the murder. The court would not consider the case against them, however, claiming there was insufficient evidence to support the charges.

In answer to these extremists in Ontario, other extremists in Quebec came to the defence of Riel and the Métis. They denied Ontario charges that the Red River Resistance had been inspired by French-Canadian Catholics and priests. They placed the blame for the troubles on the neglect of the government and on the Canadians from Ontario at Red River. Each side in this passionate debate accused the other of racial and religious prejudice. Ontario demanded that soldiers be sent to Fort Garry at once. Quebec asked that the military expedition be abandoned.

While this controversy inflamed the country, the delegates, with Father Ritchot taking the leading part, met with members of the Canadian cabinet. The government agreed to most of the clauses of the Bill of Rights. Provincial status was granted, separate schools were allowed, and an area of 1,400,000 acres was to be set aside for the halfbreeds. By May 12, 1870 the Manitoba Act, based on the Bill, under which Red River would enter Confederation, had passed through Parliament.

Ritchot was highly satisfied, even though there were two matters that troubled him. First there was the military expedition. He had hoped that troops would not be sent to Red River, but he had to be satisfied with the statement that the expedition would be one of peace. Next he wanted confirmation in writing that an amnesty would be proclaimed—that, as the Bill of Rights said, "none of the Provisional government, or any of those acting under them, [would] be in any way held liable or responsible" for the actions taken at Red River in 1869-70. As to the amnesty, the Governor-General, Sir John Young, said that this was covered in a proclamation he made on December 6, 1869, which stated that no legal proceedings would be taken against any of the Métis if they dispersed peaceably. The shrewd Ritchot was aware that this proclamation would not cover actions taken since December 1869 and particularly the execution of Thomas Scott. But the Canadian government was firm: it would provide no statement in writing promising an amnesty. The government feared the political strength of the anti-French forces in Ontario and would not commit itself. It avoided the question by stating that responsibility for granting an amnesty lay with the imperial government, since Red River was not part of Canada at the time of the insurrection. Ritchot was told that an amnesty from the imperial government would reach Red River before the arrival of the troops. Ritchot had to be content with this oral promise.

On June 17, 1870 Ritchot returned to Red River on the steamer *International*. As it docked at Fort Garry, Riel was there with a crowd of settlers to greet him. Everyone was anxious to have a first-hand account of the negotiations in Ottawa and to hear about the military expedition and the amnesty. A week after his return, on June 24, Ritchot reported what he had been told in Ottawa: that the military expedition was a peaceful one and that an amnesty would be forthcoming from the Queen. Riel was disappointed and suspicious. But he was pleased with the Manitoba Act, as were the members of the Provisional Government when they met to hear Ritchot's report in more detail. They readily accepted the Act and moved that the new Lieutenant-Governor be welcomed on his arrival. (How different from 1869 when McDougall appeared on the scene!) To the representatives gathered to hear Ritchot's report, Riel said: "If we have the happiness soon to meet the new Lieutenant-Governor, we will have time and opportunity enough to express our feelings. For the present let me say only one thing. I congratulate the people of the North-west on the happy issue of their undertakings. I congratulate them on having trust enough in the Crown of England to believe that ultimately they would obtain their rights. I must, too, congratulate the country on passing from under this provisional rule to one of a more permanent and satisfactory character. From all that can be learned, also, there is great room for congratulation in the selection of Lieutenant-Governor which has been made. For myself, it will be my duty and pleasure, more than any other, to bid the new governor welcome on his arrival. I would like to be the first to pay him the respect due to his position as Representative of the Crown."

A turning-point had been reached, and after Riel's speech

some of the men went to Emmerling's hotel and got drunk.

Riel had secured protection of the lands, the language, and the schools of his fellow Métis in Red River. He had brought representative government to the country and had fathered a new province, which came into existence on July 15. Furthermore he had been asked by Cartier in Ottawa (through Ritchot) to continue to administer the Provisional Government until the Lieutenant-Governor arrived. In the Settlement there was general satisfaction with the result of his work. Yet he was not without some doubts. On July 23 he published a proclamation from Colonel Garnet Wolseley, commander of the Red River Expedition, in which Wolseley said: "Our mission is one of peace . . ." But *was* the military expedition really a peaceful one? Riel had heard rumours that the men of the expedition wanted only vengeance. And would there be an amnesty? In Ontario they said he was a rebel and should be hanged. Could he rely on the assurances that had been given to Ritchot in Ottawa? Would the new Lieutenant-Governor, Adams G. Archibald, a French-speaking Nova Scotian, reach the Settlement and set up a government before the troops arrived?

In July, Colonel W. F. Butler visited Fort Garry on his way from Canada via St Paul to meet Wolseley's Red River Expedition, which he had been sent to join as an intelligence officer. In his famous book, *The Great Lone Land,* he describes the "desolate and ruinous" Fort: the semi-circle of mounted guns all pointed to the gate; the dirty, bare-looking white-washed buildings; the ragged-looking dusky men lounging about with their rusty bayonets; the Union Jack, "in shreds and tatters", flying with another flag bearing the fleur-de-lys and a shamrock (expressing O'Donoghue's Irish sympathies) on a white field. Butler met Riel, whom he describes as "a short, stout man with a large head, a sallow, puffy face, a sharp, restless, intelligent eye, a square-cut massive forehead overhung by a mass of long and thickly clustering hair. . . . He was dressed in a curious mixture of clothing—a black frock-coat, vest, and trousers; but the effect of this somewhat clerical costume was not a little marred by a pair of Indian mocassins, which nowhere look more out of place than on a carpeted floor."

In their conversation Butler said rumour had it that Riel was making active preparations to resist the approaching expedition of General Wolseley. Riel replied:

"Nothing", he said, "was more false than these statements. I only wish to retain power until I can resign it to a proper Government. I have done every thing for the sake of peace, and to prevent bloodshed amongst the people of this land. But they will find," he added passionately, "they will find, if they try, these people here, to put me out—they will find they cannot do it. I will keep what is mine until the proper Government arrives . . . ."

At one time, when speaking of the efforts he had made for the advantage of his country, he grew very excited, walking hastily up and down the room with theatrical attitudes and declamation, which he evidently fancied had the effect of imposing on his listener; but alas for the vanity of man, it only made him appear ridiculous; the mocassins sadly marred the exhibition of presidential power.

As the summer wore on Riel became more and more anxious. Should he leave before the troops reached Fort Garry? Should he and his followers—as one of his associates, W. B. O'Donoghue, suggested—resist the troops when they arrived? Each day the military expedition came closer to the Settlement. Yet there was no sign of Archibald nor of the amnesty promised by the Canadian government.

On the evening of August 23, 1870 the troops were camped a few miles north of Fort Garry along the Red River. That night Riel and several of his friends went out to assess the situation. "We left in a drenching rain," Riel wrote; "the weather was so dark that two men on horseback, holding each the other's hand, hardly saw each other. We were armed from head to foot. We advanced with the greatest care. . . . At last we sighted the glimmers of the fires; we pushed on far enough to distinguish the fires themselves, but it was evident that we were approaching the sentries' lines and the outposts, and, not caring to fall into their hands, we turned back." Riel slept at Fort Garry that night. In the morning James Stewart, a Company man, woke him up saying: "For the love of God, clear out! The troops are only two miles from the city and you are going to be lynched!" Bitterly Riel faced up to the fact that Wolseley's troops were not on a peaceful mission. He would have to leave the Settlement.

As the troops approached Fort Garry they expected to be fired on. But the guns at the Fort were unmanned and the gates were open. Riel was gone. The troops were disappointed that there was to be no fight. "Personally," Wolseley wrote, "I was glad that Riel did not come out and surrender, as he at one time said he would, for I could not then have hanged him as I might have done had I taken him prisoner when in arms against his sovereign." So much for the peaceful expedition.

After leaving the Fort, Riel, Ambroise Lépine, his adjutant-general, and W. B. O'Donoghue, crossed the Red River (cutting the ferry cable behind them) to St Boniface and went to see Bishop Taché. "We have fled," Riel explained to the Bishop, "because we have been deceived. We were told we had nothing to fear, but rather than run the risk of being killed or murdered we prefer to leave the fort." The three men paid a hurried visit to Riel's mother, then headed south for the United States. Riel found refuge in the Métis settlement of St Joseph, west of Pembina, in the home of Father Lefloch, who had taught him Latin in St Boniface nearly twenty years earlier. Here he waited anxiously for news from Red River. On September 6 Bishop Taché advised him by letter that it would not be safe to return.

Lieutenant-Governor Archibald arrived at Fort Garry on September 2, 1870, but without the amnesty. He found the Canadians in Winnipeg and the newly arrived militia men from Ontario a rowdy, lawless group, determined to hunt down Riel and avenge the death of Thomas Scott. "With some (I cannot say how many) of the volunteers who went up," he wrote, "a desire to avenge the murder of Scott was one of the inducements to enlist. Some of them openly stated that they had taken a vow before leaving home to pay off old scores by shooting down any Frenchman that was in any way connected with that event." There was, he found, "a frightful spirit of bigotry" among a small and hostile group in the Settlement who, he said, seemed to feel that the French halfbreeds should be wiped off the face of the globe.

Archibald, who was sympathetic to the Métis, sought to calm the situation, but his efforts at creating peace between the Canadian party and the Métis had little effect. Some Canadians tried to settle on land claimed by the Métis and an armed clash over this, and other incidents, seemed inevitable. A number of Métis were beaten or threatened. Elzéar Goulet, a member of the court martial that had condemned Scott, drowned when he was driven into the Red River and stoned by a group of soldiers and civilians. His death was investi-

gated by two magistrates but no arrests were made. François
Guillemette was killed near Pembina. André Nault, Riel's
uncle, was chased across the American frontier, stabbed, and
left on the prairie for dead.

While such enmity towards the Métis existed, Riel was wise
to avoid the Settlement. His friends advised him to stay away
for his own safety and for that of his family. Riel said he
would be patient and careful. "My life belongs to God," he
wrote to Taché. "Let him do what He wishes with it." But
Riel was never a patient man. He needed to be active, to be
involved. He ought to do something to protect his Métis
people from the Canadians and the Ontario troops. So on
September 17, 1870 he ventured into the new province of
Manitoba and at St Norbert met with a number of the Métis
leaders who drew up a "Memorial and Petition" to the
President of the United States. It charged the Canadian
government with treachery, with failing to fulfil the promise
made to Ritchot of an amnesty. It asked the United States to
undertake an investigation of the Métis grievances and to
intercede with the Queen on behalf of the Métis people for
their protection. After this petition was drafted, Riel
returned to St Joseph.

In November 1870 he was asked to be a candidate in the
first provincial election. He was tempted to stand, but when
it was suggested that it would be better to avoid political
activity for the time being, he declined the offer. This was
frustrating. Riel was the acknowledged leader of the Métis,
yet he could not represent them in the legislature. How he
longed to be in Manitoba to help his people. But he had to
remain with Lefloch, living in fear of assassination, worrying
about the safety of his family, brooding over the events that
had exiled him from his home. In February he became

seriously ill; his friends feared he would die. His mother came to nurse him but he did not improve until April.

On May 3, 1871, still weak from his illness, he returned to his mother's home at St Vital. He remained there quietly and no attempt was made to arrest him. But in September he was forced back into public life by the action of one of his associates in the recent troubles.

W. B. O'Donoghue, a tall, handsome Irishman, had taught mathematics at St Boniface College. He joined Riel in 1869 hoping he could influence the course of the Métis resistance and bring the Red River Settlement into the United States. After he fled to the United States with Riel and Ambroise Lépine, he helped draft the "Memorial and Petition" to the American President. Unknown to Riel, he revised the petition before taking it to Washington, making it read as a request on behalf of the people of Red River for annexation to the United States. In January 1871 O'Donoghue met President Ulysses S. Grant, who would not take any action on behalf of the Métis, being convinced that the request for annexation did not represent the true feelings of the people at Red River, as indeed it didn't.

O'Donoghue persisted. He went to New York and met there with leaders of the Fenian Brotherhood. The Fenian organization, seeking to gain independence for Ireland, had several times invaded Canada from the United States to attack British power in North America. Some of the Fenian leaders were ready to support O'Donoghue's plan for an invasion of Manitoba where, O'Donoghue explained, the Métis were dissatisfied with Canadian rule. He was certain the Métis would join the invading Fenians against Canadian authority. Early in October he gathered about thirty-five men at Pembina, ready to move into Manitoba. On being informed of a possible invasion, Lieutenant-Governor Archibald issued a proclamation calling on all loyal men to resist the invaders. Several companies of troops and volunteers started south toward the border.

Manitoba was in a state of alarm. Métis restlessness under the new Canadian rule was well known. Would they join the invaders? What stand would Riel take? These were the questions on everyone's mind. Riel had little difficulty in coming to a decision. First of all he assured Taché that he had played no part in organizing the invasion. "There cannot be any doubt about my conduct in this affair," he said; "it is certain that I am tied in no way with them. . . . Be sure that there is not the least danger that I or any of my friends join the Fenians. We detest the Fenians, for they are condemned by the Church, and you can be sure that I shall have nothing to do with them." Riel wanted nothing to do with O'Donoghue either. He had had several disagreements with him over the past year and suspected that the Irishman wanted to set himself up as the leader of the Métis people.

While the Fenians were gathering, Riel and the Métis leaders held a series of meetings, some of them at Riel's home. O'Donoghue had sent a message asking them to meet him at Pembina. Riel would not go but two of the Métis did—as Riel said, "in their own right", to find out what O'Donoghue wanted. They reported that he planned to seize the Hudson's Bay Company post at the border and wanted the Métis to join the invasion. The Lieutenant-Governor's proclamation had already appeared. Archibald told Ritchot that Riel's assistance against the Fenians would be looked upon with favour and that if he came forward, "he need be under no apprehension that his liberty shall be interfered with in any way . . . the co-operation of the French halfbreeds and their leaders in the support of the Crown, under the present circumstances, will be very welcome and cannot be looked upon otherwise as entitling them to most favourable consideration." Riel was convinced that the best hope for the Métis and for himself lay in loyalty to Canada. The Métis leaders agreed. They would assist the movement against the Fenian invaders. "Your Excellency may rest assured," Riel wrote to Archibald, "that without being enthusiastic, we have been devoted. So long as our services continue to be required, you may rely on us."

Early in the morning of October 5, 1871 O'Donoghue and his men dashed across the border into Manitoba and took possession of a Hudson's Bay Company post. Within a few hours American troops rounded the invaders up and marched them back to the U.S. The invasion was over before the troops from Winnipeg could reach the border and while the Métis volunteers were preparing to march.

Even though Métis assistance was not required, Archibald was relieved and gratified by their support. To show his appreciation he crossed the river to St Boniface where he reviewed the assembled Métis volunteers, met the Métis leaders, and shook hands with Riel (without acknowledging his identity). When the Canadians in Winnipeg and Ontario heard about this, they were indignant. Many of them believed that Riel had been actively engaged in plotting the invasion. They said the Métis leaders had offered their services only after the danger had passed. And for the Lieutenant-Governor to shake hands with a man they considered a rebel and a murderer was more than they could stand. They demanded that Archibald be recalled.

Having come forward with his followers in response to the call to arms, and with Archibald's assurance that his liberty

would not be interfered with, Riel might have felt more fre
to appear openly in public. But this was not the case. Th
Ontario government had offered a reward of $5,000 for hi
arrest and conviction. When the news of the Ontario offe
reached Manitoba, meetings were held in the French parishe
Riel's friends were determined he should not be forced t
leave the province again and were prepared to protect him b
armed force if necessary. While he remained in the provinc
Riel was a constant temptation to lawless men, idlers, an
roughs (as Archibald called them), who would stop at noth
ing to get hold of him and claim the reward. The danger h
was in was seen in December 1871 when several of thes
roughs broke into his mother's house. Riel was not there a
the time but the men threatened his sister Marie.

Archibald feared that Riel's presence in Manitoba migh
lead to bloodshed and was anxious to have him leave. Joh
A. Macdonald was of the same opinion. He would not gran
an amnesty, however; such an act would alienate Ontario, a
he explained to Taché (now an archbishop) on one of hi
many visits to Ottawa to wrest an amnesty from the Prim
Minister. Macdonald also did not want Riel arrested an
tried; this would alienate Quebec or force the French-Cana
dian members of his cabinet to resign. Above all the Prim
Minister wanted to hold his government together, to see th
new Confederation strengthened and extended to the Pacific
not torn apart by racial and religious emotions over Loui
Riel. To Macdonald the solution was for Riel and Ambrois
Lépine to leave the country. He asked Taché to arrange thi
and provided $1,000* for the two men and for the suppor
of the families they would leave behind. (Later, when ques
tioned about Riel by an outraged Ontarian, Macdonald said

* This amount was supplemented by $800 from Donald A. Smith.

Where is Riel? God knows. I wish I could lay my hands on him.")

Taché knew the sacrifice he was asking the men to make. Riel at first objected. "My friends would say I have been bought," he argued. But Taché convinced both men that they would be helping their own cause and that of the Métis by leaving. "Your departure would be a trial as well as a sacrifice . . . Despite that knowledge, I take it upon me to utter the painful and delicate word, Go, disappear for a time; do not leave even a pretext to those who are assailing you so unjustly."

On February 23, 1872 Riel and Lépine, with police protection, sorrowfully left their homes and headed for the United States. They went first to St Joseph, then to St Paul where Riel began to write an account of the Red River Resistance. But even in St Paul his old enemies followed him. Dr Schultz turned up in the city and offered money to a man to steal Riel's papers. Riel and Lépine overheard discussions about an attempt to arrest them for the Ontario reward. "I am uneasy," Riel wrote to Taché. "I place myself in the hands of God." Both men were depressed and lonely. News from home, eagerly sought, merely made them sad. "The Métis regret your leaving," wrote one of Riel's friends, "and wish for the day you will be with them again." His sister Marie wrote: "Your absence is hard and cruel on us." Lépine was the first to give in to loneliness. In May he returned home. The following month Riel, tempted by the suggestion from his friends in Manitoba that he run for Parliament, went back to St Joseph and finally began to campaign in the Manitoba constituency of Provencher.

Many of his friends thought it was foolish and dangerous for him to enter politics. He would be assassinated or arrested if he appeared in Ottawa. But Riel would not turn back.

Politics was in his blood now and he plunged into the
election, campaigning with great self-control against a highly
excitable opponent—Provincial Attorney-General Henry J
Clarke, who challenged Riel to a duel on one occasion. He
did not win a seat in the House of Commons in the general
election of 1872, but there is no doubt he could have won
easily had he not been asked to make another sacrifice. A
this time elections were not held on the same day throughout
the country. Before the election took place in Manitoba
George Etienne Cartier was defeated in his Montreal constitu
ency. John A. Macdonald did not want to lose Cartier and
suggested that a Manitoba constituency might be offered to
him. Riel and Clarke both declined the nomination in Proven
cher, which became open to Cartier. To Riel it seemed to be
a good bargain. If anyone would speak for the Métis and
press for the amnesty in Ottawa it was Cartier, a cabinet
minister and the leading French-Canadian politician in Can
ada. By withdrawing, it was agreed, Riel would place Cartier
under an obligation. Those who feared that Riel would only
create further divisions in the country if he were actively
engaged in politics were also satisfied. Riel could never escape
being a centre of violent controversy between Ontario and
Quebec.

In the end the bargain turned out to be a poor one. A few
months later Cartier died while visiting London. At once Riel
offered himself for the vacant seat, determined that he
should plead his own case in the House of Commons and
equally determined not to give up his seat to anyone. He was
elected by acclamation, but he had not been able to attend
his own nomination meeting because he was in hiding. Some
Canadians had decided to collect the reward that was still
being offered for his capture and a warrant was issued. Riel

heard about this from A. G. B. Bannatyne and hid out in the woods, guarded by friends. In the search for Riel, Ambroise Lépine was found and arrested.

After the election, plans were made to send Riel to Ottawa. He left Manitoba on October 21. Friends had raised money for him and selected a travelling companion, a man who could attend to the details along the way and thus relieve Riel from exposing himself unnecessarily. He arrived in Montreal six years after he had left it as an uncertain ex-student. Now he was a national figure, a member of Parliament. But in many ways he was still uncertain: he was hated by many, he had a price on his head, he was subject to arrest or assassination at any time.

Riel was soon in touch with French-Canadian politicians and journalists who had taken up his cause and they arranged for him to go to Ottawa. Approaching the Parliament Buildings, Riel gave in to his fear that if he went inside he would be seized and turned over to the police. He returned to Montreal. There, among his French-Canadian friends once more, he felt safe.

Three years of hiding and avoiding arrest had damaged Riel's health and he was advised to go to Plattsburg, New York, to stay with the Oblate Fathers. While living there he occasionally visited the French-Canadian lumbering community of Keeseville, New York, and spent many quiet hours with Fabien Barnabé, a warm, kindly priest who made him feel as if he had a home again. However, despite the comforts and the attention he received from Father Barnabé's mother and sister Evelina, Riel was lonely and very restless. He wanted to get back into political life. Another general election was to take place in Canada in February 1874 and no one could persuade him not to offer himself as a candidate in

Provencher. He did not have to return to Manitoba to cam
paign. His friends there undertook the work of the electio:
and won the seat for him.

Again he went to Ottawa. This time he found courage t
visit the office of the Clerk of the House of Commons, on
day in March, with a former schoolmate, Romuald Fiset. Th
Clerk, Alfred Patrick, who did not recognize the bearde
newcomer, allowed Riel to register as a member of Parlia
ment and take the oath of allegiance. As Riel left the room
Patrick glanced at the name on the register and looked up i
astonishment to see him bowing at the door. Leaving th
building quickly, Riel departed for Hull, across the Ottaw:
River.

The news that Louis Riel was in Ottawa spread throughou
the city. The capital was buzzing with excitement as group
of people gathered at street corners talking about the govern
ment's carelessness in allowing the rebel leader to be swor:
in, speculating about where he might be hiding, what disguis
he might be wearing, what the police would do. The new
"spread like wildfire," said a Toronto newspaper, "and in
tense excitement prevailed. A company of the Foot Guard
were ordered out who mounted guard over their armoury
while another detachment, then under arms, were kept in th
Parliament Buildings, where they could not be seen." As soo
as Riel's presence in the city had been confirmed, a warran
was sworn out for his arrest. The police began a search an
patrolled the area around the Parliament Buildings in group
of two and three. A reporter on an Ottawa newspape
claimed to have tracked down a man who said he had spoke:
with Riel. He described the Métis leader as a stout, burly
muscular man, who showed fierce determination in his eye
and countenance. On the evening of March 30, 1874, whe:

Parliament opened, the public rushed into the galleries, curious to know whether Riel would appear and take his seat. It was believed that he was already in the Parliament Buildings hiding, waiting for the session to open. Some were convinced he would be present in the galleries in disguise. "It is said", reported a newspaper "that in the crowd in the public galleries this evening there were over one hundred revolvers." As the hour for the opening of the session approached, police were on the alert on the Parliament Building grounds and throughout the building. Everyone was scrutinized and there were cases of mistaken identity—the police arrested several people they thought might be Riel in disguise.

The curiosity seekers were disappointed. Riel did not show up. Several French-Canadian members pleaded his case and demanded the amnesty, but they were unsuccessful. Riel was ordered to appear in the House. When he did not do so he was expelled as a member of Parliament.

One of Riel's most eloquent defenders at this time was young Wilfrid Laurier, sitting in the House of Commons for the first time. "How could Riel be regarded as a rebel?" Laurier asked. "What act of rebellion did he commit? Did he ever raise any other standard than the national flag? Did he ever proclaim any other authority than the sovereign authority of the Queen? No, never. His whole crime and the crime of his friends was that they wanted to be treated like British subjects and not to be bartered away like common cattle." If it had not been for the execution of Scott, he added, the events at Red River would constitute a glorious page in Canadian history. The speech did much to enhance Laurier's reputation as an orator but did little for Riel.

Ottawa and even Montreal were now considered more dangerous for Riel than Manitoba, though there was still

Louis Riel, about 1876. This photograph was reproduced on heavy card and given away as a premium by a Montreal cigar manufacturer, S. Davis and Sons, about 1876.

danger close to home. Two of his followers of the 1869-70 days had just been arrested and charged with murder and Ambroise Lépine was still awaiting trial. Riel eventually headed west but did not continue his journey home beyond St Paul. After two weeks there, and feeling very insecure, he turned back to the only place he had found peace in the years of wandering and hiding—to Father Barnabé's home in Keeseville. His wanderings had just begun, however. He was re-elected to Parliament in September 1874 but did not try to take his seat. He visited Quebec, went back to St Paul, then to Keeseville again, to French-Canadian communities in New Hampshire, and then to Washington. He was always on the move, travelling almost aimlessly, living off charity, and unable to settle down or rest. He was upset and shocked when he heard that his friend Ambroise Lépine had been sentenced to death, then relieved when just two weeks before Lépine was to be hanged—after French Canada made its indignation known in the press—the sentence was reduced to two years' imprisonment.

In Ottawa the new Liberal government headed by Alexander Mackenzie was under pressure to do something about Riel—grant an amnesty or bring him to trial. Mackenzie needed to be as cautious about Riel as Macdonald and the Conservatives had been; the Liberal party had its French-Canadian supporters as well. Like Macdonald, Mackenzie did not want to take a step that would divide the country on racial and religious lines. The decision he reached was a compromise that satisfied no one. Mackenzie's government granted Riel the amnesty it said had been promised by the Conservatives. This meant that Riel could not be tried for his part in the events of 1869-70. But the amnesty was granted on condition that he stay out of the country for five years.

4

Exile

Riel had always been a religious person. His mother was a pious woman, his home had been a devout one, and young Louis grew up in close touch with the Church and the church school. Like his father, he had been directed toward the Church as a vocation. His attachment to it was strengthened in Montreal in the 1860s when he became aware of the role it had played in the survival of French-Canadian society and the French tongue after the Conquest of 1759. The association he made between his cause and the struggle of a French-Canadian Roman Catholic minority in Canada was always present in his thinking, and he came to believe that he had a mission to protect his Church and his language, and to make the Métis people devoted to God and to the Church.

During the early days of exile Riel was tense, moody, depressed, and in a weakened state of health. His mind would wander away from reality. While he was in Washington in December 1874 he said that a spirit had visited him: "The same spirit who showed himself to Moses, in the midst of the burning cloud, appeared to me in the same manner. I was stupefied. I was astounded. The voice said to me: 'Rise up, Louis David Riel. You have a mission to perform.' I received this heavenly message with open arms and bowed head."

The following year he believed he had been given a similar

command by Bishop Ignace Bourget of Montreal, who wrote
to him saying: "God, who has always led you and assisted
you up to the present time, will not abandon you in the
darkest hours of your life. For He has given you a mission
which you must fulfil in all respects." To a man in Riel's
state of mind—to a man in exile, embittered, unrecognized,
desperate to serve but banished from his home—Bourget's
words were intensely encouraging. They gave him comfort
and hope. They gave purpose to his life and a motive for
continuing with his work on behalf of the Métis. At times
they assumed in his mind the authority of a divine command. Bourget's letter became one of his treasured posses-
sions and he carried it with him at all times for the rest of his
life.

Late in 1875 Riel was in Washington again, visiting a
French-Canadian friend, Edmond Mallet, a Métis sympathizer
who knew people of influence in the capital. On most occasions Riel was calm and reasonable. There were times, however, when he had the symptoms of a manic-depressive—becoming sublimely happy, only to be plunged into the depths
of despair shortly afterwards. One day in December, in St
Patrick's Church, he was overcome by an intense feeling of
joy and covered his face with his handkerchief to hide it from
his neighbours; then he felt a sorrow so deep that he sobbed
aloud. He would express strange notions of being a prophet
with a divine message to proclaim to the world, or outline
preposterous plans for western Canada. Through Mallet he
was introduced to President Grant. He wrote the President a
long letter in awkward English outlining a plan for re-estab-
lishing himself as head of a provisional government in Manitoba and the North West Territories. As head of such a
government, he said, he would negotiate a treaty with Canada

and set up French-Canadian and Irish provinces in the West "Mr President, if you please," he wrote, "help me to get justice for my people, the new nation, the Métis."

Mallet could not understand his friend's ideas—"I could not follow him in all his ways of thinking." He was disturbed by Riel's temper when anyone disagreed with him. He was alarmed by the emotional outbursts. Some of Riel's actions were unnatural, as when he gave away $1,000 he had received from Bishop Bourget to a blind beggar. Mallet finally became so embarrassed by his ideas and behaviour that he sent Riel to Father J. B. Primeau in Worcester, Mass. Primeau could not help Riel and was convinced that only a miracle could restore him mentally. Primeau in turn sent him to Father Evariste Richer in New Hampshire and Richer sent him to Father Barnabé in Keeseville. Though he had once spent many peaceful days in Keeseville, his condition did not change there. He frightened Barnabé's family with his crying and shouting. Barnabé was forced to contact Riel's uncle, John Lee, who took Riel back to Montreal. On the train Riel caused disturbances for which his uncle asked the passengers to excuse him, saying that Louis was just a poor lunatic. Louis saw some people laughing and cried: "Don't laugh! I am an apostle! I am a prophet!"

About six weeks later he had calmed down somewhat. His uncle gave in to Riel's pleadings to be allowed to go to church. While there he interrupted mass to contradict the priest. The church was crowded and there was a commotion while someone led Riel outside. The priest called for silence. "It is nothing," he said, "just a poor lunatic."

Riel repeatedly tore up his clothes and bed coverings and threatened to throw himself out the window, saying he wanted to go to church. When his uncle reproached him,

Louis said: "No, I am not mad! Never say that I am mad! I have a mission to fulfil and I am a prophet. Say rather that you don't understand. I am sent by God. . . ."

"At the end of a couple of months," his uncle wrote in 1886, "his madness got worse. When I saw that he had a mania for tearing up his clothes and that my wife, my servant and I were all exhausted, I got in touch with Dr Lachapelle, whom I knew to be one of his friends, to ask him if there was any way of getting him into an asylum." Riel was taken to the Hospital of St Jean de Dieu at Longue Pointe, Quebec, where he was admitted under the name of Louis R. David in March 1876. (An alias had to be used, since he was violating the terms of the 1875 amnesty by returning to Canada.) Dr Howard, who received him, described him as "a fine-looking man". "Why do you call me David?" Louis asked the doctor when he greeted him. "My name is Louis David Riel." He produced a book and showed Dr Howard his name in it. It was quickly snatched away by a nun who tore the page out. "You are known here as Monsieur David!" she said. Dr Howard wrote later: "It took us all to get Louis Riel to his room, such was his rage."

On several occasions when his uncle visited Longue Pointe he found Riel in a strait-jacket—once because he had smashed the ornaments and candles in the chapel. On another visit he found Riel standing in his cell against the wall, his arms outstretched. "He said he wished to show the nuns that he was Christ crucified. I told him to go to bed and he obeyed."

In May, Riel was transferred to an asylum in Beauport, Quebec, as Louis Larochelle. His illness was diagnosed as "delusions of grandeur". He spent much of his time scribbling verses and notes and brooding on his mission as "Louis David Riel, Prophet, Infallible Pontiff, and Priest King". He had violent periods, though visitors to the asylum found him completely calm and normal except when religion or politics entered into the conversation. So normal did he appear to some that they were convinced he was feigning madness and using the institution as a hiding-place.

Riel's health appeared to improve at Beauport and during 1877 he was allowed to visit friends outside the hospital and make short trips into the countryside. On one of these visits he met Wilfrid Laurier, the man who had defended him in the House of Commons in 1875. Laurier described him as a man of vigour, fluent, well-informed, but excitable on the subject of religion. When religion was mentioned Riel excitedly harangued his host about the great mission he had for the revelation of God's will.

He was released from Beauport in January 1878 when, according to Dr François Roy, he was cured—"more or less". Riel then went to Keeseville where he rested, following as best he could the doctor's advice that he avoid any excitement. From Keeseville he wrote to Lachapelle: "I am more obliged to you than ever. I thank you for all the trouble you have taken to help me when I was unable to help myself. I am extremely grateful for everything you did for me during the great trials to which it pleased God to subject me."

More than anything else during this period of his life Riel was helped by the attentions and companionship of Father Barnabé's sister, Evelina. The companionship developed into a love that was quiet, gentle, romantic. Soon they were secretly engaged. Riel seemed settled. He avoided politics and set out to find employment so that he would be able to support a wife. He visited New York, St Paul, and Pembina but found nothing suitable. During these trips, letters from Evelina encouraged him in his search. "My thoughts", she wrote, "are of God and you, my own dear Louis." "Pray for me," she wrote on his thirty-fifth birthday, "the one who must accompany you along the road of life." In her letters Evelina often sent him pressed flowers and in reply Riel would enclose some poetry he had written. In the spring of 1879, while he was at Pembina, she recalled for him the times he had worked around the house in Keeseville, how they had sat together on a bench in the garden and picked flowers. She also spoke of the future that lay before them and hoped she would be a worthy companion for him. At times, though, she had doubts about the future. She was not sure she had the qualities Riel expected to find in a wife. "I am a humble and not very brave woman, and I shall not be suited to the greatness of position that I should have to occupy if you are successful."

Riel was far from being a success. He had no position, no prospects, and little security to offer his Evelina. He decided he would establish himself in the western United States. Evelina was not sure she was ready to give up the quiet, dignified, comfortable surroundings of her brother's home for the rough life and hardships of the prairie. Her mother was getting old, her brother was not well. Riel thought his letters did not please her. He stopped writing and the romance ended.

A short time after his release from Beauport, Riel had written to his mother about his plan to settle in the western United States. He needed money to do this and wanted her to sell some of his lands in Manitoba. Ritchot was ready to help his mother do this, but he reported that prices were low and that the land would have to be sold at half its value. There appeared little chance that Riel would have sufficient money to set himself up as a farmer or businessman. Barnabé referred Riel to Bishop Ireland of St Paul, who wanted to bring out Catholic immigrants from the crowded cities of the eastern United States. Barnabé himself was interested in such a scheme and considered sending orphan boys to the West to be trained as farmers. Riel might be able to assist in the colonization plans. When nothing came of this Riel moved on, in the fall of 1878, from St Paul to Pembina and then to St Joseph.

In the Métis community of St Joseph Riel was close to his own people. He was also close to home but was unable to return. The reasons for his exile impelled him to pour all his resentment, his sense of injustice, of being persecuted, into a long poem that attacked John A. Macdonald. Here are a few lines from it:*

> *Sir John A. MácDonald doth govern proudly*
> *The provinces from which his power flows;*
> *While his bad faith perpetuates my woes—*
> *And all his countrymen applaud him loudly.*
>
> *Despite the peace he owes me, and despite*
> *His pledge to honour in the deed and fact*
> > *What was our Pact*
> > *And is my right,*
> *For seven years now Sir John has warred with me.*
> *A faithless man's a vulgar man, be he*
> *Either a wise man or a witling born:*
> > *And so I hold him up to scorn.*

Riel's poem, written in 1879, was not published until after his death, when it seemed pathetic, for Macdonald had by then played a much more decisive role in Riel's life than merely denying him an amnesty.

*Translated by John Glassco.

While he was living in St Joseph, Riel was able to get news easily about Manitoba politics and the development of the province. His mother and his old Métis friends, whom he had not seen since 1872, could visit him. These visits, he wrote, "filled me with joy". The news about his beloved Métis, however, did not make him happy.

Manitoba was experiencing an economic boom as thousands of settlers rushed in to take up lands offered them by the Dominion government. Winnipeg had become a city and could be reached through the United States by the railway. New towns were sprouting up all over the province. New settlers and businessmen had been attracted to the West by the possibilities of commercial farming and economic development. The new kind of life was foreign to the Métis, who had been satisfied with land enough to feed themselves or to combine their limited farm work with the buffalo hunt and employment as cartmen, tripmen, or guides with the fur brigades. But the buffalo hunt and the fur trade were fast disappearing from Manitoba. The railway and the steamboats left little business for Red River carts. The province could no longer provide the Métis with the easygoing existence they had known in the Red River Settlement and they could not adjust to the demands of commercial farming.

English-speaking settlers now formed a majority of the population of Manitoba. The French-Canadian and Métis members of the legislature had lost political influence as the number of English-speaking members increased. The denominational school system and the legal status of the French language were under attack by the now-dominant English settlers and Manitoba as a province of two languages and two cultures seemed doomed.

Many Métis believed that to the west, on the Saskatchewan

River, there was still hope for them to live the kind of life they desired. Riel learned that more and more of them were selling their land and leaving Manitoba for both the Saskatchewan plains and the Missouri River country in the western United States. He could see this exodus taking place at St Joseph, which had once been a buffalo-hunting community. Now the Métis who went out to the plains to hunt did not return. Their lands were being taken up and farmed by new settlers.

Riel had no intention of going back to Manitoba, for he was still under banishment. At the end of December 1879 he left St Joseph with a band of Métis who were planning to winter in northern Montana. For the next few years he wandered about the Milk and Missouri River country, accompanying the Métis on their buffalo hunts. There were numerous jobs to occupy him. He served the Métis as a purchasing agent. He became an Indian trader, buying goods at Fort Benton and selling to both Indians and Métis. He helped recover stolen horses. At one time he made a living as a woodchopper near Carroll. And he was constantly acting as an interpreter and intermediary for Indians and Métis with the American army and the territorial government.

While he was living near Carroll in 1881 he took as his wife a young girl called Marguerite Monet; they were married by a priest on March 6, 1882. A Métis also, Marguerite was slight, quiet, and unable to read or write. The Riels had two children: a son, Jean, born in 1882, and a daughter, Marie Angélique, born in 1883. Evelina heard about the marriage and seems to have been heartbroken, for she wrote Louis and spoke of his having destroyed her future. Louis drafted several replies but it is not known whether a letter was finally sent.

Montana was still part of the "wild west"—full of outlaws, horse thieves, and whisky traders. Wherever there was whisky, the Indians and the Métis, much to Riel's disappointment, were attracted to it. "The halfbreed", he wrote of the Montana Métis, "is a man who has a strong passion for intoxicating drinks. He spends most of his earnings in whisky. If he is a mere hunter on the prairie, liquor is one of the principal causes which make him poor and prevent him from settling. If he is trying to settle, the use of spirituous liquors empties his purse and makes him sink more rapidly into poverty, and poverty drives him away from his little farm."

Riel did not have the same influence over the Métis of the Missouri country as he had had at Red River. As leader of the Provisional Government he had been very strict with his followers. The Red River Métis had never been as dissipated as the Métis now living in Montana, who were clearly in no condition to play a part in Riel's divine mission. He tried to prosecute an agent for C.A. Broadwater and Company, which traded liquor to the Indians, and sought through the American army authorities to prevent the sale of whisky to the Métis. He failed to make a case, however. It was illegal to sell liquor to the Indians but not to the Métis, who were not Indians.

Riel's dealings in this affair with the company, headed by a prominent Democrat, and the U.S. marshall, a Republican, brought him into the rough American party politics of the time. There was an election in the Territory of Montana in 1882 and Riel supported the Republicans, who were glad to have him on their side because of his supposed influence with the Métis. The Democrats won; nevertheless Riel was accused of dishonest practices in turning the halfbreed vote against the winning candidate. When Riel defended himself in the *Helena Weekly Herald*, the affair was taken up by this paper and by the Democratic *Benton Weekly Record*. Each newspaper treated him according to its political sympathies: he was idealized by the one and maligned and scorned by the other. Riel was arrested in the end but at the trial in April 1884 the case was thrown out for lack of evidence.

In spite of the degraded conditions into which some of the Montana Métis had fallen, Riel never lost faith in them. They did not seem to understand that the days of the buffalo hunt, even on the Missouri, were fast coming to an end, and Riel thought their only hope lay in settling down and becoming farmers. If the Métis were given land and had livestock, agricultural implements, and schools, there was a chance they could improve their economic condition and adjust to changing times. Riel applied to the American government for a land grant; in return he offered Métis assistance towards pacifying the Indians of the American West. "We ask the Government", he wrote, "to kindly consider that as halfbreeds we stand between the civilized world and uncivilized man and are closely related with the several tribes of the Northwest, owing to which fact we indirectly exercise some influence and from the Indian blood in our veins we are inclined to believe that Indians will listen to us more favourably than to the majority of those who are not connected by family ties with them." But again, while the American government was eager to settle the Indians on reservations, there was no land for Métis.

The only hope for the Métis seemed to be in the Church and the mission schools, the two strong influences that had shaped the lives of the Métis at Red River. The Church, eager to help the Métis by directing them to mission settlements and schools, hoped Riel might be able to draw them to such establishments and Riel was favourably disposed to such a plan. In the spring of 1883 he became a school teacher at the mission of St Peter's on the Sun River. The position served a double purpose. Not only would he be helping the Métis but he needed employment, for he was the head of a family. Before he settled down to this new work at the mission, he became an American citizen—on March 16, 1883. Then, as the period of banishment from Canada was now over, he visited his mother and family in Manitoba.

The day after his arrival at St Vital, Riel met a large number of the Métis, who called on him at his mother's house. They still regarded him as their chief and treated him with respect and admiration. But the political leadership of the Métis and the French-speaking people of Manitoba had fallen into the hands of French Canadians from Quebec who had come to Manitoba after it became a province. Riel had little influence now. The largest newspaper in Winnipeg, the *Manitoba Free Press*, took no notice of his presence, or did not know of it, until several days after his arrival when a short item appeared on an inside page. It stated—as a second-hand report—that Louis Riel, "of insurrectionary fame", had "returned from his exile" and was expected to remain in Manitoba.

At St Vital, Riel gave a long interview to some reporters from the *Winnipeg Daily Sun*. It took place out of doors, "amid the delightful company of 1,000,000 mosquitoes", while the reporters' horses grazed under some poplars. The published interview, called "Riel's Reminiscences", opens with the words "Time works wonders", and goes on to remark that, though there would have been great excitement and a miniature rebellion if Riel had returned a few years before, now there was scarcely a ripple of interest—"And yet Riel was a most important man in the history of this new country." Though only thirteen years had passed since the Resistance, "there are thousands of people in Manitoba—in Winnipeg—who have forgotten Riel and thousands more who never knew him. . . ." Riel was wearing "a black slouched hat, beneath which was a full face with broad forehead and keen brown eyes of marked intellectuality. His black curly hair was rather shorter than that worn by the average half-breed. He has a full beard, pointed, of a darkish brown colour. He has a straight, large, prominent, well-shaped nose, and a most expressive mouth. He speaks English very well and is most particular in his choice of words. He has extraordinary self-possession, but when relating some stirring fact or exciting reminiscence, his eyes danced and glistened in a manner that riveted attention."

Here are some excerpts from the interview:

"When were you in Winnipeg last?"

"Thirteen years ago."

"Will you give us your opinion of the growth of Winnipeg?"

"I always expected that this part of British North America would be the most important point in the country, but I scarcely expected Winnipeg to prosper like it has. Its prosperity has been more than admirable."

"What is your opinion about the future of the place?"

"I think in twelve years the prosperity of Canada and the Northwest will be over. That's my honest opinion, but I may be wrong. If you make any mention of it give it as my honest opinion so that I will not be understood as slandering the country in any way."

*   *   *

"Do you think the French language will soon be dispensed with here?"

"No, I scarcely believe that. At the same time successful efforts may be made to extinguish it."

"Do you think the majority of the English-speaking people in this country will submit to the perpetuation of two languages?"

"I do not think it would be a great burden. It may bring a little conflict, but at the same time I do not see that there is any real disadvantage about it."

"Except an inconvenience?"

"To the English, perhaps, but not to the French. Besides, the continuance of the French language here was made a condition of the treaty of 1870 between the provisional Government and the halfbreed population."

"Thirteen years have passed since the troubles occurred here and time brings about wonderful changes. Now, looking at the events of that day after the lapse of thirteen years, do you now regard your action in a different light from what you did then? And if the same circumstances were to occur again, would you not act very differently?"

"I am more and more convinced every day that without a single exception I did right. Of course I don't mean to say my conduct was perfect on all occasions because every man is liable to make trifling mistakes, but had I the same thing to go through again I would do exactly the same. If the people of Canada only knew the grounds on which we acted and the circumstances under which we were, they would be most forward in acknowledging that I was right in the course I took. And I have always believed that as I have acted honestly, the time will come when the people of Canada will see and acknowledge it."

*   *   *

"Did you converse with Scott before he was executed?"

"I sent for him when he was in captivity in the Fort. I told him he was conspiring with other men. I also told him that if he had not been careful that evening, he would have been killed for trying to murder the guard we placed on him."

"Did he try to kill the guard?"

"Yes, he seized a bayonet that was in the room and endeavoured to slay the guard by plunging it into him through an opening in the door of the guard room. He was always hot-headed and violent. I will tell you of one of his crazy acts. A man named Parisien, a follower of his, was taken prisoner by us but afterwards escaped. He went back to Scott's camp near Kildonan and Scott, thinking he was a spy, took a strong scarf, tied one end around Parisien's neck and the other to the tail of his (Scott's) horse. Scott then jumped on the animal and galloped about a quarter of a mile, dragging the poor victim in this way till it was thought he was almost choked to death. He recovered sufficiently to make his escape, but Scott's followers pursued him; catching him, they beat and cut him in such a manner that he was left for dead."

"Did you speak to Scott about his attempt on the guard's life when you sent for him?"

"I told him that I could not check public opinion. I also told him the Fort was full of men exasperated at him. I told him I had no means of doing anything for him and asked him to give me his word that he would keep quiet. He replied: 'You owe me respect, I am loyal and you are rebels.' He insulted everybody and defied me. I entreated him to keep quiet but he said he would do just as he pleased and I felt convinced we could not change his mind."

"Did he ever plead for pardon?"

"No."

"Where was his body buried?"

"I have always declined to answer that question."

*   *   *

"You met Governor Archibald?"

"I met him at the Fenian raid. He knew well who I was but he pretended not to know me. . . ."

"Who introduced you?"

"I don't care to tell, but it was a gentleman now living in Winnipeg."

"What did Archibald say?"

"He pretended not to hear me."

*   *   *

"Did the Archbishop Taché advise you to go away?"

"He left me to myself and told me to do what I thought best."

"Did he tell you to go away when he gave you the thousand dollars?"

"No."

"Did he tell you from what source the money came?"

"He said it was from some friends. Had I known it was from the Dominion Government I would not have taken it. I told him that if I took any money from the Dominion Government it would be only on account of what they owed me. Because I believed the Canadian government had crushed my existence and as I acted as governor here, I considered that they were indebted to me. I served the country faithfully and instead of even thanking me I was put down as the leader of bandits. When I got the money I told Archbishop Taché that to assure myself it was not dirty money I wanted it to pass through his hands."

*   *   *

"Who was present when you signed the roll of membership and took the oath in the House of Commons?"

"Mr Patrick and Mr Fiset."

"How did you manage to get there under the circumstances?"

"I went right into the House like any other man."

"Mr Patrick knew you were going?"

"I suppose he knew something of it but it was not expected by anyone else that I would be there; in fact I did not know that morning that I would be there at noon."

"Where were you all the morning? Hidden in a committee room?"

"No, I was standing about the lobbies like any other member and I did not make any effort to keep out of the way. I just acted in an ordinary manner."

"Where did you go after you were expelled?"

"I crossed the river to Hull where I stopped seventeen days, after which I went to Lower Canada . . . ."

*   *   *

After further conversation on general topics, Riel shook hands with the reporters, "touched his hat politely, smiled, and bade his driver go on".

Riel had been home for almost a week when this report appeared on Friday, June 29, 1883.

The French-Canadian newspaper published in St Boniface did not print a word about his visit. During his first week in Manitoba the French Canadians and Métis celebrated St Jean Baptiste Day, the National Day of French Canada. Riel attended the gathering but no mention of his presence was made in the report of the celebrations nor did the main

speaker at the festivities mention his name—he who had been
one of the founders of the Manitoba branch of the St Jean
Baptiste Society in 1871.

However, Riel was more interested at this time in visiting
with his family and friends than in making public appear-
ances and arousing publicity. The visit with his mother and
his brothers and sisters was a happy one, particularly since
the marriage of his sister Henriette took place at this time.
But in several ways the trip was disappointing. Many of his
friends—former associates whom he had expected to see—had
left, as so many of the Manitoba Métis had done, for the
Saskatchewan country. Riel still needed money for the support of his family and he had expected to sell some of his
land, but land was not selling well in Manitoba. He returned
to Montana after a month as poor as ever.

The teaching position at St Peter's Mission offered Riel a
settled life. He enjoyed teaching and was a good teacher. But
he was unhappy. The salary was small. The Riels, who had to
share a cabin with the family of James Swan, lived in "one
corner of his little house". Louis had to devote much of his
free time after school to his pupils, the Indian and Métis
children; this was time he would have preferred to spend
writing poetry and discussing politics and religion. He had
thought he could be useful to the Métis as a teacher but the
children showed little progress and their parents were not
interested in settling down. "I have not been well . . . ," he
wrote in June 1884. "My health suffers from the fatiguing
regularity of having to look after children from 6 in the
morning until 8 at night, on Sunday as well as on the days of
the week. I am interested in the progress of the children and
in the welfare of the school. I have its success at heart. And
in consequence I try to do my best. I do not know if my

work is worth very much; but I do it conscientiously. I do not get enough rest." The job of teaching school was frustrating to a man who sought a more active career, who had a mission to fulfil.

News from his family did not help to cheer Riel. His land could not be sold, money was scarce in Manitoba, there were fever and diphtheria throughout the province, and his sister Sara, a nun at Ile à la Crosse in northern Saskatchewan, had died after a long illness. Yet he longed for family news, to know how his mother was and how the crops were doing. "Your letters", he wrote, "are helpful and consoling amid the troubles which overwhelm me. Let us pray and be prepared for the next life."

On June 4, 1884, Riel was called out of church because visitors had arrived from Canada to see him. He had been expecting them and knew what they wanted. The month before he had received a letter informing him that a delegation from the North Saskatchewan country would be visiting him. The letter told of Métis grievances and said that agitation was developing against the Canadian government. "We may say", the letter read, "that the part of the North-West in which we are living is like Manitoba before the troubles, with the difference that there are more people, that they understand things better, and that they are more determined; you will form an idea as to the conditions upon which the people base their claims for the reason that there are many people in the North-West whom the Government have recognized less than Indians; yet it is these poor halfbreeds who have always defended the North-West at the price of their blood. . . . They have been petitioning for the last ten years. . . . Do not imagine that you will begin work when you get here; I tell you it is all done, the thing is decided; it is your presence that is needed. . . . The whole race is calling for you!"

The delegation, representing the French and English half-breeds of the North Saskatchewan country, consisted of Moise Ouellette, Michel Dumas, James Isbister, and Gabriel Dumont, the leader of a buffalo camp that had developed into the community of St Laurent. The visitors did little more than outline further the grievances against the Canadian government and extend an invitation to Riel to come to their aid. Riel was flattered to think that he was not forgotten by the Métis and that he was considered the only man who could lead them. He asked for time to consider the invitation, but he had already made up his mind. It was as Bishop Bourget had said: he had a mission to fulfil. Here was the opportunity. Here was God's plan for him and the Métis people.

5

Grievances

Those Métis who had left Manitoba after 1870 to follow the buffalo hunt in the Northwest had formed a number of small mission settlements—such as Qu'Appelle, Batoche, Duck Lake, and St Albert—in the Saskatchewan country. They were joined by other Métis who had lived in the Territories for many years around the fur-trade posts. Their life was an unsettled one, alternating between the shifting buffalo-hunt camps and small river lots near the missions to which they returned each winter. The buffalo were becoming scarce and these settlements became more and more like permanent homes. The situation in the North West Territories in 1884 was in many ways similar to that in the Red River Settlement in 1869. The Métis feared the advance of agricultural settlement to the area, for it was bringing with it changes to their traditional way of life.

Under the Manitoba Act of 1870 the Dominion government had set aside close to a million and a half acres within the province for distribution to the families of halfbreed residents. There were complexities and confusion before this land could be allotted and the halfbreeds became increasingly irritated by continuing delays. First a census had to be taken to determine who was entitled to a grant. Then there were changes in the government regulations, further delays, and another census. It was nine years before all the land was distributed. In the meantime many of the Métis had left the province, angered by the delays and by the fact that settlers from eastern Canada were allowed to take up land before the halfbreed claims were settled.

The halfbreeds thought that the grant was the government's way of recognizing their rights to the land because they were part Indian. The government had never intended this recognition. Because such rights seemed to be recognized in Manitoba, however, the halfbreeds outside the province believed they were entitled to a similar grant. Those in the North West Territories first petitioned the government for a grant in 1873. As the number of Métis from Manitoba increased and as white settlements began to develop beyond Manitoba, the question became more urgent. French, English, and Scottish halfbreeds were united in the demand for a grant similar to that given to the halfbreeds in Manitoba.

Under legislation passed in 1878 the federal cabinet was given authority to grant the land but it did not proceed. The halfbreeds continued to agitate and forward petitions, to which the government merely replied that the question of a land grant was still being considered. Year after year the same request was made and still no action was taken. The government ignored the demand even when it came from the North West Territories Council. In 1882, almost ten years after the first petition had been sent to Ottawa, the government replied: "The condition of the Half-Breed population of the Territories, and the claims which have been preferred on their behalf to be dealt with somewhat similarly to those of the Half-Breeds of the Red River, have been receiving careful consideration, with a view to meeting them reasonably."

It was true: the government *had* given the matter consideration. And it had sought advice. But it could not decide how to deal with the demand. John A. Macdonald thought the halfbreeds might be treated as Indians and given reserves, or

be given land as the white settlers were, under the Homestead
Laws. He was opposed to giving them scrip, or a paper title to
land, for, as he pointed out, when this was done in Manitoba
the halfbreeds had often sold it for very little. In the end,
nothing was done to satisfy the halfbreed demand for land.
Or rather, what was done came too late. In the spring of
1885, faced with the outbreak of rebellion in the North West
Territories, the government quickly appointed a commission
to investigate the question.

The Métis had other grievances. They wanted French-
speaking land agents, surveyors, and magistrates. They
wanted greater recognition of themselves as a distinct and
separate people and greater representation on the North West
Territories Council. "It is a crying shame", complained David
Laird, the Lieutenant-Governor, "that the halfbreeds have
been ignored. It will result in trouble and is most unjust."
Bishop Vital Grandin of St Albert wrote to a cabinet minister
in 1884 saying: "The members of the government ought not
to ignore the Métis. They, as well as the Indians, have their
national pride. They like to have attention paid to them and
could not be more irritated by the contempt of which they
feel themselves rightly or wrongly the victims."

When government surveyors moved into the Territories,
the halfbreeds wondered if they would be given legal title to
the small plots of land they already occupied. Would their
long river lots running back from the water be wiped out by
the government's system of square surveys? Would they have
to fulfil the requirements demanded of new settlers under the
Homestead Laws? Petitions were sent to Ottawa.

The Dominion government again said it would give consideration to these petitions, but little was done. The halfbreeds
continued to hold meetings, to agitate the question, to for-

ward more petitions. In 1884 the government finally moved. It began an investigation of the claims, but the report, made by a Land Inspector, was lost or ignored in Ottawa until the spring of 1885 when rebellion threatened. When the rebellion broke out, the Liberals (who had themselves paid little attention to the grievances when they were in office between 1873 and 1878) charged Macdonald and the Conservatives with neglect and mismanagement of North West Territories affairs. In defending the Conservatives, one cabinet minister went so far as to say that no statement of grievances had ever been received by the government!

By 1884, when Riel returned to Canada, there were, in addition to English and French halfbreed settlements, a number of white settlements in the North West Territories. One of these was Prince Albert, which had been established on the North Saskatchewan River as a Presbyterian mission and had grown considerably as settlers from eastern Canada moved west. "Within the last five years", one newspaper editor wrote of Prince Albert in 1878, "the settlement of which Prince Albert forms the centre has been making giant strides towards the goal of civilization and agricultural improvement. The buffalo hunter is rapidly giving way to the farmer, and the Indian trader to the merchant."

The changes around Prince Albert were typical of the developments feared by the Métis. By 1884 newspapers were being printed at Prince Albert, Battleford (the capital of the Territories until 1883), and Edmonton. These settlements were connected by a telegraph line and could be reached by steamboat. Canadian surveyors were everywhere along the North Saskatchewan River. By 1883 more than sixty million acres had been surveyed for homesteaders. North West Mounted Police posts dotted the western plains. And the Canadian

Pacific Railway, though much to the south of these settl
ments, would be completed to the Pacific coast in 1885. Th
railway was bringing in more settlers from the East and alon
this steel trail new settlements developed: Regina, Moos
Jaw, Medicine Hat, and Calgary. To white settlers all thes
changes represented progress and economic development bu
to halfbreeds and Indians they were serious threats to the
established way of life.

As white settlement penetrated lands once frequented onl
by the buffalo hunter and the fur trader, the Indians becam
alarmed. The fur trade had moved northward; the buffal
had been driven west and south. Indians found their means c
livelihood and food supply rapidly diminishing. By 1877 th
Canadian government had negotiated seven treaties with th
Indians of Manitoba and the North West Territories, coverin
the area from Lake of the Woods to the Rocky Mountain
The first was signed with the Cree in a ceremony at Lowe
Fort Garry in 1871 and the seventh with the Blackfoot i
what is now southern Alberta.

All the treaties were much the same. In return for th
surrender of their land the Dominion government set asid
reserves for the exclusive use of the Indians; a money pay
ment or annuity was to be given to each Indian; schools an
teachers were to be provided; agricultural implements, live
stock, and farm instruction promised; and sometimes a hors
and wagon were given to each chief. The bargain was not
good one, considering the later value of the land surrendered

The government wanted to see the Indians give up thei
wandering life and settle down in agricultural communitie
where they would be able to provide for themselves; thei
land was needed for the expected number of homesteaders
The Indians were unable to resist the advance of an agricul

ural society. They were not a well-organized group and could do little else but come to terms with the changing life on the western plains. They were aware that the days were gone when the buffalo thundered by the thousands across the prairies, raising clouds of dust.

Not all the Indians co-operated with the government's program of having them sign treaties, settle down, and accept reserves. Some chiefs, such as Big Bear, an influential Cree who lived near Fort Pitt, refused to sign a treaty at first, preferring the freedom of roaming the praires in search of buffalo to the life of a farmer or rancher. Faced with the scarcity of food, however, most chiefs were eventually forced to agree to the terms of the treaty and bring their wandering bands to a reserve. They had struggled for their independence, for the right to follow the life they and their ancestors had known, but their cause was a lost one. That world was gone and there was little they could do to change the course of events. Big Bear settled down near Battleford, but he refused to go to a reserve.

Very few of the Indians were able to cultivate the land successfully. With no experience as farmers, most failed in the attempt. The government had told them they would be able to provide for themselves on the reserves, but the change from hunter to farmer was not an easy one and their efforts were not productive. Those who left the reserve in search of a buffalo herd, hoping to provide food and clothing for themselves, found nothing. They would then return to the reserve in a wretched condition, close to starvation, and have to call on the Indian agent for food allowances to keep themselves alive. In 1882 a North West Mounted Police inspector wrote from Fort Walsh: "There is a great deal of misery in all the camps owing to the old women and children being housed in

wretched cotton lodges, which are no protection whatever i
cold weather; their clothing is poor and the only means the
have of living is the small issue of food they are at presen
receiving from the Government." In 1883 the Dominio
government's need for economy cut down the amount c
food available and the already considerable distress and hard
ship suffered by the Indians were increased. That year one c
the Indian agents described his Stony Indians as "mere skele
tons".

The government had expected too much from the Indian:
It did not understand what it was like for an Indian to chang
his whole pattern of life, to change from one kind of societ
to another. When the Indians found they could not provid
for themselves on the reserves, and when the government cu
food allowances, the Indians charged that government offi
cials had not kept faith with them. They claimed that th
promises made had been broken. Missionaries and Mounte
Police, who were well aware of the growing unrest among th
tribes, were sympathetic and did not approve of the goverr
ment's economy measures, believing that the policy woul
lead to an Indian uprising. If the policy of false econom
continued, wrote Superintendent L. N. F. Crozier of th
North West Mounted Police, "there is only one other [po]
icy] and that is to fight them." There already had bee
isolated instances of Indians breaking into food warehouse
and several skirmishes with Indian agents and the police

The police were watching closely for any movement of th
Indians out of their reserves. In particular they kept an ey
on Big Bear and Poundmaker, another Cree chief, who had
been persuaded to settle on the Battle River. Both chief
were moving about the plains attempting to combine th
Indian tribes into one united force to press their grievance

against the government. At a gathering of Indians at Duck Lake, Big Bear expressed his sadness at the new way of life that was being forced on them and called for action on the part of all the tribes to express their dissatisfaction and resentment. He did not attempt to organize the Indians for war. He sought rather a great confederation of the tribes: from a united and strengthened position they could better speak to the government to force improved terms under the treaties. Yet fears of an Indian uprising spread throughout the white settlements.

Once Riel returned to the Northwest, the police believed he was responsible for arousing the Indians and for leading them in their agitation. Certainly Hayter Reed, the Indian Commissioner, saw Riel's influence behind the Indian movement. With little sympathy toward the Indians' plight, he wrote:

Big Bear is an agitator and always has been, and having received the moral support of the half-breed community, he is only too glad to have an opportunity of inciting the Indians to make fresh and exorbitant demands. There are Indian as well as white agitators and the hard times make one and all, good and bad, only too prone to give any assistance they can towards procuring more from the authorities without having to work for it. Riel's movement has a great deal to do with the demands of the Indians, and there is no possible doubt but that they, as well as the half-breeds, are beginning to look up to him as one who will be the means of curing all their ills and obtaining for them all they demand.

Hayter Reed sounds like the kind of person on whom Sir John A. Macdonald relied for his opinions about the condition of the North West Territories. The West was important to Macdonald and to his policy of building a united and

strong transcontinental nation. To hold the West within Co>
federation, he was aware, the Canadian Pacific Railwa
would have to be supported and completed. The railwa
would hold the West, and the West would make a railwa
pay. During these years, however, the CPR was in difficulty
It never seemed to have enough money to continue its wor
and was constantly in search of further loans and fund
Macdonald was so occupied with the important problem c
the railway and with trying to hold his government togethe
in the face of continued opposition to his policies that he wa
unable to give to the West the attention it demanded. Be
sides, he tended to discount rumours and statements abou
unrest in the North West Territories. He put the blame fo
these and for the unrest itself on a few troublemakers lik
"land sharks" and land speculators who, he said, wanted th
Métis to have land so they themselves could get their hand
on it. As for the Indians, Big Bear and Piapot, another chie
were just "Indian loafers". He was aware of unrest among th
Indians but did not think they would start anything unles
there was a halfbreed or white uprising.

White settlers too had many grievances against the Domin
ion government. Most had not found the prosperity they ha
expected when they came west. There was a burst of eco
nomic activity after 1879 but some who had bought lan(
hoping to sell it at increased prices lost everything in 188.
when the land boom collapsed and prices fell. At the sam
time the price of wheat dropped and an economic depressio
left settlers burdened with debts. Agriculture was faced wit
further setbacks by drought and frost. The tariff on farn
machinery, intended to protect eastern manufacturers fron
foreign competition, kept the cost of machines high. Th
CPR had a monopoly—the government would not allow com

peting lines. Farmers were angered by the rates the railway charged for carrying their grain to outside markets. Discontented farmers, like the halfbreeds, began to hold meetings; a farm organization was set up and petitions to the government were drafted. The farmers wanted lower tariffs and railway rates. They asked for a railway to Hudson Bay. They objected to land regulations and timber dues. And they wanted representation of the North West Territories in Parliament.

The newspapers in the West supported these demands. One paper likened the situation to the days of Charles I and vowed that the people of the West would not submit to taxation without representation. In 1884 the Prince Albert newspaper said: "The people of Manitoba and the North-West Territories have for a long time past been struggling by every legitimate means in their power to impress upon the Eastern Provinces the fact that they have been treated with deliberate and gross injustice, and that however anxious they may be to avoid extreme measures, they will not shrink, should the worst come to the worst, from taking any steps absolutely necessary for the vindication of their rights."

English and French halfbreeds, white settlers, and Indians were united—all had grievances against the Dominion government and were demanding action. In May 1884, in a schoolhouse at Red Deer Hill, southwest of Prince Albert, representatives of these groups met to discuss the situation. One of the questions debated was whether they should consult Riel. There were some objections to such a move but finally the meeting agreed to invite Riel to assist them in bringing their grievances to the attention of the Dominion government. It was as a result of this meeting that Moise Ouellette, Michel Dumas, James Isbister, and Gabriel Dumont visited Riel at St Peter's Mission in Montana.

6
Agitation

Louis and Marguerite Riel packed up their few belongings and with their two children set out for the Saskatchewan country in Canada on June 10, 1884. They moved slowly through Sun River for the last time, accompanied by the wagons of the Saskatchewan delegates. On their way out of town Riel stopped to give an interview to the editor of the *Sun River Sun*. He told him he was going north to help his people but that he would return. The editor had been a member of Wolseley's expedition in 1870. "It was queer to sit and talk to this man", he wrote, "and remember how as a drummer boy of fifteen we longed to spill his blood."

Three weeks after leaving Montana, they were met at Fish Creek in the Saskatchewan country by an enthusiastic welcoming party of about fifty wagons. The next day they arrived at the Métis village of Batoche, where the Riels stayed with Louis's cousin, Charles Nolin, for the next four months.

The man who had fought and suffered for the Métis, their chief, had returned. But the Métis were not the only people who welcomed Riel. "I have been received with open arms by everybody," he wrote to his brother Joseph; "the English halfbreeds extend the hand of welcome to me. The Upper Canadians [the people from Ontario] declare themselves for me." Riel was surprised when several men whom he had imprisoned at Fort Garry nearly fifteen years before invited him to visit them. He was pleased to see again his old friend and close associate of 1869-70, Louis Schmidt, who was now working in the Land Office at Prince Albert. Schmidt was excited and optimistic about Riel's return and moved by the thought that "he who had been master in his own land . . . now returned as a homeless stranger". "May it be his intention", Schmidt wrote to the newspaper *Le Manitoba*, "to remain permanently in our midst. This man can do nothing but good for his compatriots, and he is the only one who will obtain everybody's support in any kind of a dispute. His is a great name among the French and English halfbreeds, and it is undeniable that his influence, well directed, will be of immense assistance to them."

On July 11, 1884 Riel and several of the Métis leaders visited Red Deer Hill to meet with English halfbreed and white settlers, several hundred of whom turned out to hear him speak. Again he was accepted enthusiastically. He had made no passionate or fiery speeches to the Métis in Batoche and he made no attempt to excite the people at Red Deer Hill. He was satisfied at this stage to be calm and moderate and to call for unity. At this meeting he met W. H. Jackson, secretary of the Settlers' Union, an agricultural association of white settlers formed the year before to organize the agitation against the government. Riel found that Jackson and other white settlers were hot-headed and impatient, and far more fired up about taking action than he was. One newspaper in the Northwest had openly suggested that rebellion was the only way the country would get attention from Ottawa. Frank Oliver, editor of the Edmonton *Bulletin*, wrote: "If it was not by—not threatening, but actual—rebellion and appeals to the British government for justice that the

people of Ontario gained the rights they enjoy today and
freed themselves from a condition precisely similar to that
into which the North-West is being rapidly forced, how was
it? If history is to be taken as a guide, what could be plainer
than that without rebellion the people of the North-West
need expect nothing, while with rebellion, successful or
otherwise, they may reasonably expect to get their rights."
These were strong words compared with the moderate and
restrained speeches Riel gave when he began meeting the
people of the Saskatchewan country.

Many settlers were not convinced that Riel's purpose and
method were as innocent as they appeared. Once a rebel
always a rebel was their attitude. One newspaper could see no
reason for calling on Riel and said: "We cannot believe the
Government will seriously entertain any claims or proposi-
tions put forward by or through Riel." Many believed, like
this newspaper, that Riel would only harm the cause. Riel
was hesitant, therefore, when a group of Prince Albert settlers invited him to address a public meeting there. He had
reason for alarm. A Hudson's Bay Company man warned
Father Alexis André of Prince Albert that the prejudice
against Riel in the settlement might lead to friction. Father
André passed this opinion on to Riel and recommended that
the Métis leader avoid the meeting. Riel accepted this advice
and in response to the invitation he had received replied that,
while he felt he would be safe from discourtesy, he thought it
best to postpone the meeting "for the sake of avoiding even
the slightest trouble" and "to allow no germ of division to
weaken our basis of agitation." The postponement was for a
short time only. The invitation was presented again. This
time André approved. You are "the most popular man in the
country," he wrote to Riel; "everyone awaits you with impa-

ience." André must have admitted this reluctantly for he did not approve of Riel's return and believed that his presence would not be in the best interest of the Métis or the Church.

Not everyone in Prince Albert was sympathetic to Riel but nearly everyone turned out to see and hear him on July 19. Though he spoke in English—he was much more fluent in French—he warmed his audience with his charm and sincerity. To many, however, his speech was a disappointment. They expected him to excite and arouse them with his words. Instead he called for the unity of all races in the Northwest. He referred to grievances: the Indians, he maintained, had been robbed by the advance of civilization; the halfbreeds could not compete with the people from eastern Canada. But he was calm and moderate. He urged all his listeners to combine in a unified effort to obtain free title to their land and provincial status for the Districts of Saskatchewan, Assiniboia, and Alberta or elected representation of these districts in the federal Parliament. He did not recommend bold action or violence, however, because he was for peace, "believing that the object would be gained faster if they acted orderly and peaceably".

The opposition that André had at first feared did not develop—though one man stood up and called Riel a criminal, but he was thrown out of the meeting.

Riel was happy with the results of his initial meetings with the halfbreeds and the white settlers. Now he was active again, at the very centre of things and the leader of a political agitation. "Not long ago," he wrote to his family in Manitoba, "I was a humble schoolmaster on the far-away banks of the Missouri, and here I am today in the ranks of the most popular public men in the Saskatchewan." He attributed this change in the fortunes of his life to God.

Organization of the Northwest movement proceeded on an orderly basis. Each group, halfbreeds and white settlers, continued the agitation among its own people and a central committee was set up to co-ordinate activities. Local committees were organized to hold public meetings and draw up lists of grievances. All of these were to be considered by the central committee and incorporated into a petition to the Dominion government.

Riel took charge of organizing the Métis and met with those Indian leaders who sought his advice. Jackson organized branches of the Settlers' Union and worked to make Riel more acceptable to white settlers. A Liberal opponent of Sir John A. Macdonald, Jackson used every opportunity to embarrass Macdonald's government and to place blame for conditions in the Northwest on the Conservative party. Like westerners in later years, he criticized the Dominion government for supporting what he called "eastern interests". He argued that the federal government did not understand western problems and ignored western demands. The West should have representation in Parliament where its voice could be heard. "Possibly we may settle up with the East and form a separate federation of our own in direct connection with the Crown."

Jackson was stating grievances that western newspapers had been repeating for years—and often in a more threatening tone. Yet as the direction of the agitation fell more and more into Riel's hands the newspapers became apprehensive. While Jackson was recommending Riel to the white settlers, the newspapers were countering his efforts. They hesitated in their support of Riel and, particularly after he met with Big Bear and other Indian chiefs, they began to warn the public to be wary. Rumours and reports, often exaggerated, spread throughout the country that Riel was encouraging rebellion among the Indians and was planning to use the threat of an Indian uprising to promote his own cause. As fear of an Indian war increased, the initial cordial feeling among the white settlers toward Riel changed. Riel's enthusiasm at the reception he had received was premature. He still had to face much opposition, not the least of which was the attitude of the Roman Catholic clergy.

Riel had hoped he would find active support for his cause among the clergy, as he had done in 1869-70. But in 1884-5 there was no Ritchot on whom he could count as an ally and supporter. Now the clergy were suspicious of him. Not that they were unsympathetic to the Métis people and their cause, but the more Riel gained the unquestioning and devoted worship of his people, the less influence the clergy had with them. André did not approve of Riel's sense of his "divine mission" and called him a "fanatic".

Riel was annoyed at the failure of the clergy to support him and reacted with foolish emotional outbursts, charging them with being in alliance with the government against the Métis. On one occasion he accused them of being spies for the North West Mounted Police. He said that he was losing faith in the clergy and began to question their authority in Church and religious matters.

In September 1884 the Bishop of St Albert, Monseigneur Vital Grandin, paid a visit to St Laurent, where the Riels were living with Moise Ouellette. Riel complained to the bishop that the clergy were not supporting him. Bishop Grandin countered with the complaint that the Métis had not taken the clergy into their confidence or kept them informed of actions planned. Riel did not want a breach with the clergy for he feared this would lead to the withdrawal of Métis

Louis Riel, about 1884

support, so he suggested the organization of a Métis society that would have the blessing of the church, and the celebration of a religious holiday that would be associated specifically with the Métis people. The bishop agreed to these suggestions. St Joseph was chosen as the patron saint of the Métis and a special mass was held at St Laurent to celebrate the organization of the Métis society, called the Union Métisse de St Joseph. Riel believed that he had forged, with the Church's blessing, a union between race and religion. "Now we are established as a nation," he declared to a crowd of rapt Métis at the end of the celebration on September 24.

Riel then turned to the work of preparing the petition for Ottawa. Before it was ready he and Jackson saw an opportunity to present the grievances of the Northwest in person to Sir Hector Langevin, a member of the federal cabinet who was visiting the North West Territories. They hoped Langevin would come to Prince Albert, but the cabinet minister would not go beyond Regina. Had he met with them he might have been able to take back first-hand information to the government in Ottawa. He refused to make the trip, however, and the opportunity passed.

By the middle of December 1884 the petition was ready. It dealt with the grievances of the Indians, the halfbreeds, and the white settlers in the Northwest, outlining the problems that had led to unrest and agitation. It repeated charges made in petitions that had been sent to Ottawa since 1873: the Indians were unable to provide for themselves; the halfbreeds had not been given a grant of land and did not have a title to the land they occupied; white settlers wanted changes in the land regulations and a railway to Hudson Bay, one that could compete with the CPR and give them cheaper access to the European market.

Riel could not resist including criticism of the Canadian government that dated back to the Red River Resistance. The petition referred to the arrest of the delegates of the Provisional Government of Manitoba when they went to Ottawa in 1870; it charged the federal government with failing to live up to the terms of the Manitoba Act. Manitoba and the Northwest had become, it said, "a mere appendage" of Canada. Canada had not given them control of their lands or resources and it had not given the North West Territories representation in Parliament. It asked the government to organize the Saskatchewan district as a province. Finally, it asked permission to send delegates to Ottawa to discuss the petition "whereby an understanding may be arrived at as to their entry into Confederation, with the constitution of a free province."

Receipt of the petition was acknowledged promptly by the Secretary of State, Adolphe Chapleau. (John A. Macdonald later claimed that no such petition had ever been received, even though it had been acknowledged by a member of his cabinet and a copy sent to the Colonial Office in London.)

With the petition off to Ottawa, Riel began to think about going back to Montana. The work he had said he would do was completed. Many of the clergy would have been delighted to see him go. They were uneasy about the influence he had over the Métis people, some of whom, one priest said, looked upon him as "a Joshua, a prophet, even as a saint". Riel had questioned the authority of the clergy; he had criticized them for failing to support him. And he had such strange religious ideas: they wondered about his sanity when he suggested that he wanted to set up an independent nation in the Northwest with his own religion and a supreme pontiff. The clergy were sympathetic enough to understand Riel's feelings of oppression. They could understand his outburst of temper and the feelings of suffering and misfortune that Riel said resulted from his years of exile. But they questioned his mental stability and were convinced he should leave the country. They suggested that the government assist him financially, as it had done after the Red River Resistance. Father André wrote to Lieutenant-Governor Dewdney: "I think it is really the duty of the government to get Riel out of mischief as soon as possible . . . the presence of that man in the country will be a source of anxiety to the government, and we do not know what may happen at last."

Riel had no means of supporting himself and his family. He was dependent on others for his needs, as he had been for most of his life, and in the Northwest he relied on money collected by friends on his behalf. He did not like living on charity and had hoped, he said, that he would have "a fair living" some day. He felt he had claims on the government. Was he not entitled to a grant of land, as all halfbreeds were under the Manitoba Act? Had he not brought Manitoba into Confederation? Did he not save it from the Fenians in 1871? And had he not passed up a seat in Parliament in favour of George Etienne Cartier when asked to do so by the government? Was he not, therefore, entitled to some compensation for these sacrifices? "For fifteen years," he said, "I have been neglecting myself. My wife and children are without means, while I am working more than any representative in the North-West. Although I am simply a guest of this country—a guest of the halfbreeds of the Saskatchewan—although as a simple guest I worked to better the condition of the people of Saskatchewan at the risk of my life, to better the condition of the people of the North-West, I have never had any pay."

Father André believed that he would respond favourably to the suggestion that he leave the country if funds were provided for him. But Macdonald, who had been prepared to forward money to get Riel out of Manitoba after 1870, now looked upon Riel's claim as blackmail. He was convinced that Riel's only purpose in returning to the Northwest had been "to extract money from the public purse". The Prime Minister would not pay Riel to leave the country.

Macdonald misunderstood the mood of the halfbreeds, he misjudged the influence Riel had with them, and he underestimated the grievances of the Northwest. There were rumours of discontent, he wrote to Donald A. Smith, but "I don't attach much importance to these rumours." Early in 1885, however, Macdonald approved the appointment of a commission to investigate the halfbreed claim to a land grant, and he had already made plans to strengthen the North West Mounted Police.

Neither the halfbreeds nor Riel were calmed by the news of a commission to investigate the claim for a land grant. They had heard such promises before. As yet there had been no reply to the petition or to the request that delegates go to Ottawa, and Riel was annoyed that no attention had been paid to his personal claim for consideration.

Riel's Métis followers would not hear of his leaving. At one public meeting he suggested that his work was finished. It might be better, he said, for the Métis cause if he did leave, since the government might be more disposed to deal with grievances if he were not involved. To the suggestion that he leave, his followers cried: "No! No!" One community of Métis wrote to him offering their respect and affection. They called him "the true father of the French people of the North West, the valiant tribune . . . , the true founder of Manitoba" who, with God's help, could not but triumph. "We are convinced you will be one of the renowned men of our century; it is glorious to have a leader such as you. God will make you successful." Riel decided not to return to Montana.

Convinced of his divinely inspired mission to lead the Métis people, Riel now became more emotional and more belligerent in words and actions. Since the Dominion government had paid no attention to the list of grievances or to his own claim, Riel was determined to show the government how dangerous it was to ignore the people of the Northwest. He was certain he could count on the support of the Métis, even if the clergy were opposed to him. In March 1885 he decided that more aggressive steps had to be taken and hinted that rebellion might be necessary. To his close associates he said that if they were to save the country from "evil government" they must be prepared to take up arms. The clergy were alarmed at this turn of events. From the pulpit on March 15 Father Fourmond condemned armed resistance to constituted authority and threatened to deny the sacraments to anyone who took part in an uprising, thus evoking a stormy protest from Riel, who was present at the church in St Laurent when this sermon was preached. Riel now began to talk openly to the halfbreeds and others about striking "a blow to gain their rights". He boasted about the support he had throughout the Northwest and he even claimed that he could call on the Métis and the Indians of the United States. "The time has now come", he said, "to rule this country or perish in the attempt."

The change in the direction of the movement and the excitement that Riel was arousing among the halfbreeds were noted by the North West Mounted Police and the government officials in the country. Everything Riel said and every movement he made was reported to Ottawa. Superintendent Crozier of the Mounted Police warned the government that the Métis were talking about attacking Fort Carlton. When some of Riel's Métis followers heard that police were on their way to reinforce the fort, they lost control of themselves. On their way to tell Riel on March 18, they burst into Kerr's store near Batoche and took some government officials, including an Indian agent, prisoner. Then at Batoche Riel led them as they stormed the Walters and Baker store.

"Well, gentlemen, it has commenced," Riel said as he strode into the store.

"What has commenced?" said Mr Walters.

"Oh, this movement for the rights of the country."

They then proceeded to help themselves to ammunition and provisions.

Also at Batoche Riel announced that a Provisional Government had been established. He told Father Fourmond that Rome had fallen and that there was a new Pope—Bishop Bourget. "You will be the first priest of the new religion and henceforth you will obey me." "Never!" said the priest. However on the 19th Riel proceeded to pick officers for his council, which he called the Exovedate—a pseudo-Latin word meaning "those picked from the flock". The small Métis mob—whose activities on this day were unknown to the majority of the Métis—yelled their approval of each appointment.

Riel's temperament was as unstable as ever. One moment he would say that all he wanted to do was make a show of force or, in his own words, "to make a demonstration of strength" against the government. Then he would become violent, crying out that what the Métis were after was blood —"We want blood! It is a war of extermination! Everybody that is against us is to be driven out of the country!" These outbursts of temper, which were usually followed by calm apologies, were outward signs of the emotional instability that worried the clergy, who were unable to accept Riel's leadership of the Métis or his religious ideas.

The Métis themselves had begun to wonder about many of Riel's strange notions, but on the whole they supported him. He was one of them and had fought before on their behalf. He was the only possible leader of their cause.

As for the English-speaking halfbreeds and the many white settlers, they had welcomed Riel to the Northwest and they had supported him, though with some hesitation, while he directed the agitation against the government along peaceful lines. But they drew back when he began to mix religious reforms with the movement to redress grievances and especially when he talked about rebellion. Part of their alarm was caused by distrust of his influence with the Indians and by fear of an Indian war. In surprisingly moderate language, considering his excited state at the time, Riel appealed to both groups for support in what he called the "bold but just uprising". "The government", he wrote, "has been maliciously ignoring the rights of the original halfbreeds during fifteen years. The petitions which have been sent to that Government on that matter and concerning the grievances which our classes have against its policy are not listened to: moreover, the Dominion has taken the high-handed way of answering peaceable complaints by dispatching and reinforcing their Mounted Police. . . . The original halfbreeds are determined to save their rights or to perish at once. . . . Let us all be firm in the support of right, humane and courageous . . . just and equitable in our views, thus God and man will be with us and we will be successful."

The white settlers responded to Riel's plea by organizing militia units and calling on volunteers to be prepared for an expected attack on their communities by Riel or the Indians. The English-speaking halfbreeds, on the other hand, though they disapproved of the aggressive stand Riel was taking, would not organize to oppose him. They would not make any hostile move, preferring to remain neutral. Riel pleaded with them in a letter of March 23: "A strong union between the French and English halfbreeds is the only guarantee that there will be no bloodshed." But as one of them said: "It is dangerous to resort to arms." Instead the English-speaking halfbreeds were content to draft yet another petition.

The affairs in the Northwest were approaching a climax and Riel was moving quickly toward a course of action that would arouse violent passions against him throughout the whole of Canada. On March 21, 1885 he and his council demanded the surrender of Fort Carlton on the North Saskatchewan River. Riel believed that if he took the Fort he would "bring the Government to terms". At this time the Fort was occupied by Superintendent Crozier with a force of Mounted Police and volunteers from the white settlement at Prince Albert. Riel's demand was made in a letter to Crozier, who was told to declare his agreement to surrender in these words: "Because I love my neighbour as myself, for the sake of God, and to prevent bloodshed, and principally the war of extermination which threatens the country, I agree to the above conditions of surrender." A refusal would mean an attack by Riel and his men and the beginning of a "war of extermination".

Crozier declined to surrender. He was expecting a reinforcement of 100 men to arrive from Regina.

On March 26, Crozier decided to send out a small detachment in a dozen sleighs to get some provisions from a store at Duck Lake, about fourteen miles away. Near Duck Lake the detachment met thirty or forty armed Métis led by Gabriel Dumont, Riel's adjutant-general, who jumped off his horse and loaded and cocked his rifle. Heated words were exchanged with Thomas McKay, a Scottish halfbreed—Dumont threatened to blow his brains out—and some Métis went into the sleighs and tried unsuccessfully to snatch the lines of the teamsters. Dumont fired his rifle into the air, but he and his men then stepped off the road and the sleighs were allowed to return to Fort Carlton.

In the meantime Crozier, hearing that his detachment had been intercepted, marched out of the Fort with every policeman and volunteer available and a small cannon. It was a foolish move. He should have waited at the Fort which, with the reinforcements expected shortly, would not have been attacked by the Métis. Commissioner A. G. Irvine of the Police, who was leading the reinforcements, thought that Crozier had been impetuous and showed bad judgement.

Before Crozier reached Duck Lake, Riel arrived with a body of 300 Métis on horseback and a few Indians. Both Dumont and Riel were surprised when the police appeared. The Métis, thinking they were to be attacked, sent out Isidore Dumont and an Indian with a white blanket indicating that they wished to talk. Crozier and an interpreter advanced to meet them. The Indian seized the interpreter's rifle and the two struggled. Crozier, seeing the Métis force advancing on his flanks and believing he was being out-manoeuvred, gave an order to fire. C. P. Mulvaney describes what happened next:

The rebels had now mostly left the road and were getting under cover among the bluffs or groves in front of our men,

Gabriel Dumont, probably taken when he was an attraction with Buffalo Bill's Wild West Show

and even around their flank. A number made their way into an empty log building to the right of our line, from which they poured a murderous fire on the volunteers. The cannon fired three shots; then, by a sad mistake, a shell was put in before the charge of powder, and the gun became useless until the engagement was over. The rebels' fire was very severe. Our men were in a hollow, while the enemy had good cover and higher ground. The Indians and halfbreeds fired with great coolness, dropping on their blankets and taking sure aim. They were gradually working round the flank of our force and about surrounding it when orders were given to retreat. A rush was made for the road; the teams were hitched up; the wounded, with the exception of one man who was not noticed, had already been put in the sleighs; and the force retreated, leaving nine men dead or dying on the field.

Three years later Gabriel Dumont recalled the flight:

They had to go through a clearing so I lay in wait for them, saying to my men: "Courage, I'm going to make the red coats jump in their carts with some rifle shots." And then I laughed, not because I took any pleasure in killing but to give courage to my men.

Since I was eager to knock off some of the red coats, I never thought to keep under cover and a shot came and gashed the top of my head, where a deep scar can still be seen. I fell down on the ground and my horse, which was also wounded, went right over me as it tried to get away.... When Joseph Delorme saw me fall again, he cried out that I was killed. I said to him: "Courage! As long as you haven't lost your head, you're not dead!"...

While we were fighting, Riel was on horseback, exposed to the gunfire, and with no weapon but the crucifix which he held in his hand.

The Métis, with superior numbers, and under the military leadership of Gabriel Dumont, had forced the police and the volunteers to retreat after a battle lasting about thirty minutes. Twelve of Crozier's force were killed. The Métis lost five, including Gabriel Dumont's brother Isidore.

After the battle Riel gathered the Métis force together and called on them to "Give three cheers—Hurrah for Gabriel Dumont! Thank God who gave you so valiant a leader!"

The Mounted Police abandoned Fort Carlton and with the volunteers returned to PrinceAlbert. The Métis were convinced, as Riel was, that God had given them their victory. Riel's stature was raised immensely in their eyes. The Exovedate council passed a resolution recognizing their leader's claim "as a prophet in the service of Jesus Christ".

Riel did not plan to follow up the victory at Duck Lake with an attack on other positions. He thought of the battle as an unfortunate accident and still wanted to get the support of other groups in the country. He hoped to bring united pressure to bear on the Canadian government and to discuss the matters dealt with in the petition. He wrote to Crozier asking him to assure the volunteers at Prince Albert that he did not want to fight them; he wanted their support in establishing a government. In his letter he blamed Crozier for the battle. "A calamity has fallen upon the country yesterday," he said. "You are responsible for it before God and man. Your men cannot claim that their intentions were peaceable since they were bringing along cannons. And they fired many shots first. God has been pleased to grant us the victory; and as our movement is to save our lives, our victory is good, and we offer it to the Almighty."

7
Rebel or Hero?

Riel looked upon the battle at Duck Lake as self-defence. White settlers and the rest of Canada saw it as the opening of an armed rebellion. Whatever sympathy people had for the Métis and their grievances Riel had damaged by resorting to arms. He damaged it further when he appealed to the Indians, following the battle, to assist him. The defeat of the Mounted Police increased his prestige among the Indians and had been the signal for some of them to show their strength. On March 30, stores and buildings at Battleford were broken into by Poundmaker's Indians and the settlers were forced to take shelter in the Police barracks. At Eagle Hills the Stony Indians killed a farm instructor. At Frog Lake, on April 2, Wandering Spirit, with a band of Big Bear's Crees, murdered the Indian agent, several white men, and two priests. White settlers throughout the Northwest were terrified.

Riel's messages spurred the Indians and Métis to further acts of violence. He wrote to the Indians and Métis at Battleford saying: "The police have attacked us, we met and God gave us the victory. . . . Rise: face the enemy, and if you can do so, take Battleford—destroy it." In another message to the Métis he said: "Be ready for everything, take the Indians with you. Gather them from every side. Take all the ammunition you can, whatsoever storehouses it may be in. Murmur, growl, and threaten. Stir up the Indians. Render the police of Fort Pitt and Battleford powerless."

Though some Métis were alarmed by Riel's belligerence and deserted him, most accepted him as an inspired religious leader and "looked upon him as a saint and an angel descended from heaven," in the words of Father Fourmond. The priests, who were restricted in their movements by Riel, were forced to agree to be neutral. They could do nothing but listen helplessly while Riel harangued the Métis, giving voice to his contempt for priests who called the taking up of arms for a sacred cause a rebellion.

Any hope that the Canadian government would agree to receive delegates to discuss the Northwest petition was now gone. Canada's only answer could be troops. Troops had defeated the "rebel" in 1870 and Riel had been forced to flee when Wolseley appeared. Now troops would have to be sent again. With the news of Duck Lake and the fall of Fort Pitt, which was burned by Big Bear's Crees, Canada demanded action. Even those newspapers that had criticized Macdonald's government for its neglect of the Métis now resolved that an armed force was necessary to put down the rebellion. The Toronto *Globe* expressed sorrow that a peaceful adjustment of the Métis grievances was not possible. The government was to blame, it said, for the Métis had a "strong claim to our kindest consideration". "The rebellion", said a Montreal newspaper, "can and must be crushed out, no matter what the expense. It must be taught the halfbreeds and Indians of the Northwest that the whole power and resources of Canada will be utilised for the protection of settlers in the Northwest, and it is imperative that the lesson should be taught [so] that it will be remembered for all time to come."

Even before this outcry demanding action, the government

had decided on a show of armed might. Instructions were sent to strengthen the Mounted Police in the Saskatchewan country. Major-General Frederick Middleton, head of the Canadian militia, was sent to Winnipeg; and orders were issued for the mobilization of some Canadian militia units. The news from Duck Lake confirmed the necessity for these preparations and hastened the recruiting of men from all parts of Canada. Before the Métis force led by Riel was crushed, close to 8,000 men had been enrolled.

Middleton's plan was to move north with his force from Fort Qu'Appelle, near Regina, toward Batoche, the Métis headquarters. Another force, under Major-General T. B. Strange, was to move north from Calgary, toward Edmonton, attack the Indians on the North Saskatchewan River west of Batoche, and then move eastward to join Middleton's men. A third force, under Colonel William Otter, was sent north from Swift Current to relieve Battleford where the people of that settlement had taken refuge in the Mounted Police Barracks and were surrounded by Indians.

Middleton, dressed in a buffalo-skin coat and a fur service cap, left Fort Qu'Appelle with about 400 men on April 6, 1885. His progress was slow, for the bitter cold and hail and sleet hindered the movement of his force and equipment. By April 16 he had reached Clarke's Crossing on the south branch of the Saskatchewan River about forty miles south of Batoche. On the 17th he was joined by men of the Royal Grenadiers, bringing his strength to 800. At Clarke's Crossing he divided his force in two. One column was to cross the river and march toward Batoche on the west side of the river; the other was to advance on the east side.

Riel was not caught unawares. His Indian and Métis scouts had kept an eye on Middleton's troops from the time they left Fort Qu'Appelle. Preparations were made to resist the troops but Riel and Gabriel Dumont could not agree on a battle plan. Dumont, a buffalo hunter all his life, was a man of action. He was still suffering from the wound he had received at Duck Lake but he was anxious to go out at once, if not to attack Middleton at least to harass his men all night long—"to demoralize them," he said, "and make them lose heart." Dumont's plan was to play for time, to slow the progress of the troops and give the Indians time to arrive. Riel did not approve of this direct action; he thought it better to wait at Batoche. He had been assured through prayer, he said, that the Métis would emerge successful if the troops attacked.

Dumont was uneasy. He thought his own plan was a better one, yet at first he accepted Riel's decision. But he was eager to go and so were his men. Finally Riel gave in to him. With Dumont he rode out at dusk from his Batoche headquarters on April 23, at the head of his Métis troops and some Indian allies. When they were eight miles from Batoche they received word that Mounted Police from Prince Albert were coming by the Qu'Appelle road to surprise Batoche. Dumont sent fifty of the Métis back with Riel, then proceeded with his plan to ambush Middleton's men.

Dumont had about 150 men with him. At daybreak they caught sight of Middleton and his force encamped near a farmhouse.

I thought it wise to retire and go and wait for the enemy at Fish Creek Coulee, known among us as Little Beaver River. . . . The Tourond family lived on the right bank of this stream. . . .

I set out about four in the morning with Napoléon Naud to reconnoitre the enemy camp and I went ahead about half a mile from the place where I left him. I dismounted on a piece of high ground. As I saw the enemy scouts pursuing our scouts, I tried to draw them into the woods. I heard them sounding the bugle, but they didn't dare to follow us.

We returned to the Touronds' place where I had a bull killed for breakfast.

Around seven o'clock a scout, Gilbert Berland, warned us that a column of about 800 men was advancing upon us. I therefore placed 130 of my men in a hollow on the left bank of Fish Creek, opposite the Touronds' house, and I had the horses hidden in the woods. I left with 20 horsemen to take cover further ahead along the path to be followed by the troops with the idea of not charging them until they should be thrust back by the others, and I gave orders to my principal force not to attack them until they were all in the coulee.* I wanted to treat them as we would buffalo. . . .

An English halfbreed scout appeared and Dumont shot at him and plunged down into the coulee. Middleton's men then began firing, at twenty past seven, while several of Dumont's twenty horsemen fled to join the larger force. Dumont returned fire.

When they saw I was making things too hot for them they began directing their shots into the thicket where I was. The breaking of the branches all around me warned me that it wasn't wise to stay there. I don't know if I killed many men because I took cover immediately after each shot, but I couldn't have missed often.

One of his Sioux allies, in war paint, foolishly danced up a slope shouting a war cry and was shot down. Dumont climbed up to get his weapons and found him lying on the ground singing. "I asked him if he were mortally wounded. He said no."

A coulee is a shallow ravine.

The bullets of Middleton's men, who were hiding in the surrounding clumps of trees, were now whistling from both sides of the coulee. Dumont decided to rejoin the main body of his men, of whom there were now only forty-seven, most of the rest having fled.

We went down into a hollow in the prairie which was closer to the enemy lines. I saw an officer who was aiming at us. I hastened to finish him off and our young men began to laugh derisively when they heard him crying like a child.

We kept them in check all day because I kept firing hard, and so that I could do so more quickly the young fellows about me kept supplying me with cartridges, which were rapidly becoming exhausted. When I saw there were only seven cartridges left, I decided to set fire to the prairie grass to make the enemy, who found themselves facing the wind, withdraw. I figured on going, under cover of smoke, to pick up the ammunition and arms which they would abandon in their flight. I instructed my men to shout and sing during this operation.

Dumont then tried to get back to the forty-seven men in the coulee but found that they were surrounded by enemy fire.

Not being able to rejoin them, I returned towards the men remaining in the clump of trees on the prairie. My Sioux had slipped away from me and I found myself with only seven men. I tried again to reach the men fighting in the coulee, but it was impossible for me to go there without exposing myself to certain death.

I took my seven companions to eat at Calixte Tourond's house. It was sundown.

Middleton had had superior numbers and firing power but he failed to press his advantage because he was unsure of what strength Dumont might have in reserve. Neither side

won a decisive victory at Fish Creek. Casualties were ligh
The Métis lost four men, Middleton's force about fifty
Middleton was satisfied with the performance of his untrie
troops, however, and with the Métis retreat to Batoche
Dumont believed he had slowed Middleton's progress towar
Batoche and that he had gained time to gather together
stronger force.

When Riel got back to Batoche he learned that the rumou
of a Mounted Police advance from Prince Albert was a fals
one. He was at his headquarters when the battle began an
could hear Middleton's cannon. "I attribute our success t
Riel's prayers," Dumont said later. During the engagemen
Riel prayed with his arms stretched out to form a cross
When his arms tired, some Métis held them up.

Middleton's advance had been halted only temporarily. O
May 7 he started out again towards Batoche. Two day
later the final battle of the North West Rebellion between th
Métis and the Canadian troops began. One of the strange
parts of Middleton's attack was the use of an armed gun-boa
on the Saskatchewan River. This was the steamer *Northcote*
which was used normally on the river to supply Hudson's Ba
Company posts. It was converted into a floating barricade
armed with a gatling gun* and manned by a force of fightin
men. The gatling gun was placed on the forward upper dec
ready for action. The sides of the boat were barricaded an
strengthened (with wood and planks taken from Dumont'
barn, six miles south of Batoche) and the cabin made bulle
proof by medicine chests, boxes, and mattresses. Lashed t
the sides were two barges each loaded with supplies. Aroun
the barge decks were piled bags of flour and oats behin

* A machine gun developed in the American Civil War, here used for the first tim
in Canada.

which the men could take cover and fire on Batoche.

The *Northcote* was to be used to bring supplies and ammunition to Middleton and to attack Batoche from the river at the same time Middleton was attacking from land. But everything went wrong from the outset of this "naval expedition". Métis scouts were watching as it was made ready for its trip downriver and were well aware of what the plan was. The captain and the crew had never been down that part of the river before and were unfamiliar with the currents and sandbars.

On the morning of May 9, the day of Middleton's attack, the *Northcote* was approaching the settlement ready to play its part in the battle. Unfortunately, however, the pre-arranged signals between the steamer and Middleton's force had become confused and the *Northcote* began its attack an hour too soon. Dumont was ready. About 175 of his Métis were on the hill in front of the town. The rest, about thirty, he placed opposite Batoche church.

Since the boat . . . had to pass through a rapid caused by a bend in the river before it could continue on its way, I had suggested that at this spot we cripple the helmsman so as to set the boat adrift, and that an iron cable, thrown across the river, would make the vessel capsize.

My men did in fact fire on those who were on deck and several of them threw themselves into the water. And the boat, as I had foreseen, went adrift. I galloped on horseback along the bank to give the signal to lower the cable, but it was done too slowly; the cable only caught the funnel, which was torn away, and a fire started. The crew, however, extinguished it, although my men fired on any that showed themselves on deck.

While they fired, the Métis cheered and the Indians

shouted war whoops. Before Middleton's troops had ever arrived, the *Northcote* was floating helplessly downstream past its target.

For three days a Métis force of about 300 obstinately withstood the large Canadian force. According to Dumont, "Riel walked about unarmed in front of the lines, encouraging the fighters."

When the troops entered Batoche, they numbered several thousand; our men had at first fallen back half a mile. I myself stayed on the high ground with six of my brave fellows. I held up the advance of the enemy for an hour. What kept me at my post, I must admit, was the courage of old Ouellet. Several times I said to him: "Father, we must retreat." And the old fellow replied: "Wait a minute! I want to kill another Englishman!" Then I said: "All right, let us die here."*

When he was hit, I thanked him for his courage, but could not stay there any longer . . . .

On May 12, their ammunition almost gone, the Métis were forced to scatter into the surrounding countryside. When Dumont met Riel in the woods, Riel said: "What are we going to do? We are beaten." Dumont replied: "We must die. You must have known that in taking up arms we would be defeated." Batoche had fallen to the enemy, but Dumont was not ready to give up—he still had a few cartridges he wanted to fire. Riel, however, knew that the end had come. He had not wanted to fight Middleton's men. He had wanted to negotiate, but it was too late for compromises.

As the white flags of surrender began to appear on the roofs of the Métis homes, Dumont set out to obtain food, blankets, and horses for an escape. Then for four days he

* José Ouellette, Dumont's ninety-three-year-old father-in-law.

poked for Riel but could not find him. On hearing that Riel had given himself up, he set off to the south towards the United States. "The good Lord did not wish me to see poor Riel again. I wanted to advise him not to surrender; but he might well have won me over to his way of thinking." It was May 16.

The rebellion had collapsed, though the Indians to the west were still under arms. Colonel Otter had relieved Battleford on April 30. He then met Poundmaker at Cut Knife Hill on May 2 and was forced to retire to Battleford. Big Bear's Indians met General Strange's force at Frenchman's Butte near Fort Pitt. Because of disagreements among the Indians, there was only a short engagement and they dispersed in the night of May 28. Meanwhile Middleton had left Batoche for Battleford where Poundmaker, who had learned that Riel had been captured, surrendered to him on May 26.

Riel had sent his wife and children to a friend's home across the river from Batoche and on May 13 he wrote to Middleton: "My council are dispersed. I wish you would let them go quiet and free. . . . Would I go to Batoche, who is going to receive me? I will go to fulfil God's will." The same day he gave himself up to three Mounted Police scouts and was taken to the headquarters of Middleton, who later described the meeting:

As soon as Riel arrived in camp he was brought to my tent while one was being pitched for him next my own. I found him a mild-spoken and mild-looking man, with a short brown beard and an uneasy frightened look about his eyes, which gradually disappeared as I talked with him. He had no coat on, and looked cold and forlorn, and as it was still chilly out of the sun I commenced proceedings by giving him a military great coat of my own. He spoke English perfectly, and I had

a long talk with him. He told me that he had intende
escaping to the United States with Gabriel Dumont, bu
finding troops all about in the woods he had given up th
idea of doing so, as he felt he could not bear the hardship
and privations he would have had to undergo in trying t
escape, not being accustomed to a hunter's life as Dumon
was.

After conversing with Riel a good deal for two days,
came to the conclusion that he was sane enough in genera
everyday subjects, but was imbued with a strong, morbia
religious feeling, mingled with intense personal vanity.

After giving him some dinner I sent him off to his tent an
placed him under the personal charge of Captain Young,* th
Brigade-Major, who never let him out of his sight until he ha
handed him over to the Police Authorities at Regina, eve
sleeping under the same blankets with him.

On May 17, under guard, Riel was taken to the jail in th
North West Mounted Police barracks in Regina, where h
arrived on May 23. He made plans at once for his brothe
Joseph to go to Batoche and take his wife and children bacl
to Manitoba. Within a short time he heard from his mother
telling him of her grief, bidding him to have courage and t
look to heaven for refuge and consolation. Riel replied
asking his family to pray for him. "Do not be distressed, m
dear Mother. Bid my brothers and sisters to place all thei
confidence in God, have the children pray fervently. I know
well that I am not forgotten in their prayers. But to redoubl
their devotions pray together evening and morning." Rie
tried to explain his actions in the rebellion and asked hi

* Captain George Young was the son of the clergyman who attended Thomas Scot
at his execution in 1870.

Riel as a prisoner, May 1885. He was photographed by Captain James Peters, when he was allowed out of his tent. C.P. Mulvaney tells us that "Riel looked askance at the 'instantaneous' camera, perhaps fearing that it was an infernal machine, but as it didn't go off, he walked back into his tented prison apparently well pleased."

mother to send him some shoes, a shirt, a coat, and som
money for stamps.

Riel was in jail for eight weeks before he was brought t
trial. He busied himself with letters to his family and witl
writing prayers, visions, and prophecies in his notebooks. H
also wrote to Lieutenant-Governor Dewdney and the Prim
Minister. "Ah, my pen!" he exclaimed in his notebook. ""
have great need that you should be skilled! The people t
whom you write are so distinguished." In one letter t
Macdonald he said he hoped he could return to political lif
in Manitoba as a cabinet minister.

Meanwhile a Riel Defence Committee was set up in Que
bec to engage three lawyers—François Lemieux, Charles Fitz
patrick, and J. N. Greenshields—to go to Regina to plead fo
him. Riel proceeded to inform his lawyers of the backgroun
of his case: that he had been invited to the Northwest by th
Métis, that he and the Métis had always been on the defensive
that he had freely given himself up to Middleton in the end
The lawyers decided that they had only one chance of saving
him. There seemed to be no hope of clearing him of th
charge of having taken up arms against the government. Afte
talking to Riel and hearing him speak of his mission, hi
visions, his religious ideas, they decided to plead insanity.

In July 1885 all of Canada's attention was focused or
Regina in anticipation of the news of the trial. At one time
known as "Pile of Bones" because of the accumulation o
buffalo bones in the area, Regina was only a few years old as
the capital of the North West Territories. Sightseers anc
newspapermen crowded into the town hoping to catch a view
of the famous prisoner and to report on the proceedings o
the trial. The place was so overcrowded that the three hotel:
could not handle the visitors. One hotel-keeper took over a

store next to his hotel and fitted it up with sleeping accommodations. Would Riel and his "red allies" in war be introduced to the hangman's knot?* That was the question everyone was asking.

The trial opened on July 20, 1885 in a makeshift courtroom that had been set up in a business block, since a court house had not yet been built. The Mounted Police, fearing the Métis might try to free Riel on the way to the courtroom, dressed him in one of their own uniforms and took him to his trial in a carriage. The courtroom was crowded with curiosity seekers come to see the "rebel", the "murderer" of Thomas Scott. The clerk of the court read the charge against him, which was high treason. When asked how he pleaded, Riel answered: "I have the honour to answer the court I am not guilty." Riel's lawyers managed to obtain a week's delay in the proceedings to enable them to bring witnesses to Regina. They would have liked, for instance, to call Dumont if the government would grant him protection, but this could not be guaranteed.

The trial began on the 28th and a jury of six men—not one a French Canadian or a Métis—was chosen. One of the Crown lawyers who was to argue the case against Riel stated that the evidence to be presented would show that the so-called patriot and leader of an oppressed people had come to the Northwest not so much to help the Métis but to use them "for his own selfish ends", that he was seeking power and money, that "he desired blood . . . and was altogether reckless of the means he employed to further his ends."

The Crown lawyers produced witnesses and evidence intended to support this charge. Much of the evidence was damaging to Riel's position, especially the statements he had made

Both Poundmaker and Big Bear were brought to trial and given short sentences.

about a war of extermination against the Métis's enemies. As witnesses appeared, Riel's lawyers attempted to get from them statements about his religious ideas, his visions and prophecies. They wanted evidence to prove Riel's emotional instability. Riel did not approve of this approach and was unhappy with his lawyers' tactics. He tried to give them advice but they ignored it. He tried to interrupt the court proceedings to question witnesses himself but was told that only his lawyers could do that: he would be allowed to speak later.

"If you will allow me, your honour," he protested to Judge Hugh Richardson, "this case comes to be extraordinary, and while the Crown, with the great talents they have at its service, are trying to show I am guilty . . . my good friends and lawyers, who have been sent here by friends whom I respect, are trying to show that I am insane." He had many questions he wanted to ask the witnesses. His lawyers were not able to ask the right questions, he said. They had to put questions to men with whom they were not acquainted about circumstances they did not know. The judge ordered him to stop interrupting: he must leave the conduct of the case to his lawyers. If he persisted in trying to question witnesses, his lawyers warned, they would withdraw from the case. Riel gave in reluctantly but protested: "I cannot abandon my dignity. Here I have to defend myself against the accusation of high treason, or I have to consent to the animal life of an asylum. I don't care much about animal life if I am not allowed to carry with it the moral existence of an intellectual being."

On the witness stand his uncle, Charles Nolin, claimed that Riel had taken advantage of Métis ignorance and passed himself off as a prophet. Other witnesses supplied evidence that he had aroused the Indians and called on them for assistance. Some mentioned his temper and his outbursts against anyone who opposed him. He was not a devout man, Father André testified; he merely pretended to be a sincere religious person to gain control of the Métis people. Whenever religion or politics was discussed he was a "fool", he did not have "his intelligence of mind", he was not "responsible": he seemed to be two men and lost all control of himself on these questions. Father Fourmond said much the same thing: "In private conversation he was affable, polite, pleasant, and charitable to me. I noticed that even when he was quietly talked to about the affairs of politics and government, and he was not contradicted, he was quite rational; but as soon as he was contradicted on these subjects, then he became a different man and would be carried away with his feelings."

A number of doctors were called to provide evidence about Riel's state of mind. Dr François Roy of the Beauport Hospital in Quebec—who had known Riel when he had been confined there but had not examined him or seen him since that time—was of the opinion that "his mind was unsound . . . he was not in a position to be master of his acts." Dr Daniel Clark of the Toronto Asylum thought Riel "was quite capable of distinguishing right from wrong". Dr James Wallace of Hamilton, who had examined Riel in jail for half an hour, testified that he had not discovered any insanity—"I think he is of sound mind," he said. Dr A. Jukes, a Mounted Police surgeon, had seen Riel almost every day in the jail at Regina. He had never made any special study of insanity and his evidence could not be called expert testimony. But during his visits with Riel he had never noticed anything to indicate that Riel was insane.

When all the evidence had been presented, Charles Fitz-patrick addressed the jury in Riel's defence. He gave a strong, emotional speech, discussing the grievances of the Métis, the need for change, Riel's poverty, his desire to act within constitutional bounds, and most importantly his mental illness. Judge Richardson then asked if Riel had any remarks to make to the jury. Throughout the trial Riel had appeared impatient, at times pacing back and forth within the confined space of the prisoner's box. He had wanted to take a direct part in questioning witnesses but the court had prevented this. Now he had an opportunity to state his own case in his own way. He began with an apology. "I cannot speak English very well," he said, "but am trying to do so, because most of those here speak English." (No one on the jury understood French.) After asking God to bless the court, the jury, and his lawyers, he set out to defend himself against the charges made and the contention that he was insane. Though he had difficulties with English he spoke clearly, often eloquently, at times bringing his clenched fists down on the railing of the prisoner's box.

"The day of my birth," he said, "I was helpless and my mother took care of me. . . . Today, although a man, I am as helpless before this court . . . as I was helpless on the knees of my mother the day of my birth. The North West is also my mother, it is my mother country . . . and I am sure that my mother country will not kill me . . . because a mother is always a mother, and even if I have my faults, if she can see I am true, she will be full of love for me." He outlined the attempts he had made to unite the people of the Northwest and to direct the attention of the government to their grievances. "No one can say", he continued, "that the North West was not suffering last year . . . but what I have done, and risked, and to which I have exposed myself, rested certainly on the conviction I had to do, was called upon to do something for my country." He maintained that the agitation in the Northwest would still be constitutional if the Métis had not been attacked by the Mounted Police. "I know that through the grace of God," he cried, "I am the founder of Manitoba." He insisted again as he had for years that he had a mission and with God's help had passed through many dangers. God, he felt, was still protecting him. God was helping him to prove he was not insane, helping him to wipe away the stain on his reputation because he had been in an asylum, where he said he always believed he had been put "without reason". If he were hanged he knew it would be because he had been judged a sane man. He did not want to be remembered as an insane person. "Even if I was going to be sentenced by you, gentlemen of the jury, I have the satisfaction if I die—that if I die I will not be reputed by all men as insane, as a lunatic. . . . Gentlemen of the jury, my reputation, my liberty, my life are at your discretion."

Riel spoke for over an hour and when he had finished he was exhausted. He had repeated himself—dealing with one point, then moving on to another, and going back over the first—but he had made a passionate and effective speech, one that gained much sympathy for him in the courtroom.

It might have been the speech that convicted him. If he sounded confused to his listeners, he did not sound like a lunatic. He had taken up arms against the government; that could not be denied, even though he might seek to show there was justification for such action. If he were going to clear himself of the charge of treason he would have to show, as his lawyers believed, that he was of unsound mind. Riel was too proud a man to let his mission be blemished by the

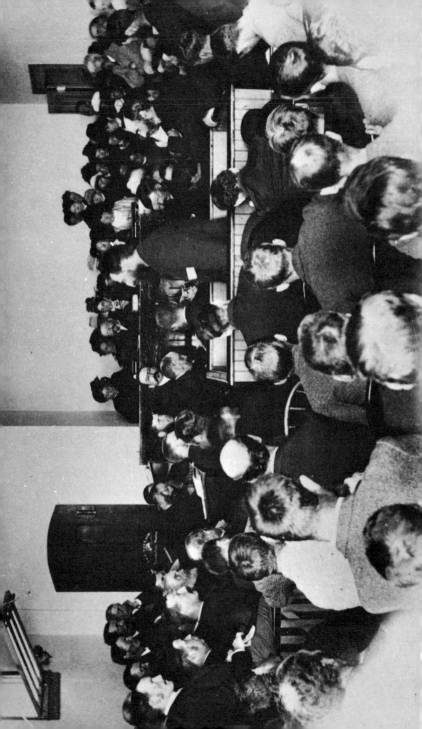

suggestion that he was a fool. He was the leader of the Métis people, the father of Manitoba, and he would not have his cause remembered as the work of a lunatic.

Riel was followed by Christopher Robinson for the Crown. In summing up the charges against Riel, Robinson dealt extensively with the question of Riel's sanity. He pointed out that the doctors who had appeared as witnesses had testified that they saw no signs of an unsound mind. His most effective points were made with the questions: How could an insane person have led six or seven hundred men into rebellion unless they also were all insane? How could the Métis live with Riel for eighteen months without detecting his insanity? The question of insanity, Robinson insisted, had to be dismissed. Riel had taken up arms against the government, he had incited the Indians, and he must be judged as a sane man for the crimes he had committed. If Riel's scheme had succeeded, he said as he finished his address to the jury, "if these Indians had been roused, can any man with a human heart contemplate without a shudder the atrocities, the cruelties which would have overspread this land. . . . Those who are guilty of this rebellion . . . must suffer the punishment . . . of the crime of treason."

On July 31, in the late afternoon, Judge Richardson began to address the jury, outlining to them the law in regard to high treason. Their duty, he charged, was to consider two points. First, had the charge of treason been proven? If it had, they must then decide whether Riel was "answerable". That is, was he of sound mind and could he be held responsible for his acts? He explained what the law was in regard to "legal insanity". It was simply a question of whether a man knew right from wrong.

When the judge had finished his charge the next day, the

jury retired. They were out for only an hour, during which time the spectators chatted excitedly, reporters milled about, and Riel's voice could be heard praying. When the jury returned, Riel rose from his kneeling position. "Gentlemen," said the Clerk of the Court, "are you agreed upon your verdict? How say you, is the prisoner guilty or not guilty?" "The jury find the prisoner guilty," was the answer. The foreman of the jury added: "I have been asked by my brother jurors to recommend the prisoner to the mercy of the Crown." When the verdict was announced, many in the court bowed their heads in sorrow. There was no rejoicing. The jury too, by their recommendation, indicated the sympathy they had for the man on trial for his life.

Riel had remained calm as the jury reported. When asked if he had anything to say before sentence was pronounced, he replied firmly: "Yes, your honour." Again he made a speech —a long, confused, rambling one in which he had to stop several times because, as he said, he felt weak. He had been found guilty of high treason, yet this verdict gave him some satisfaction, for the verdict meant he had been considered sane. "I suppose", he said, "that, after having been condemned, I will cease to be called a fool, and for me it is a great advantage. . . . I would not be executed as an insane man. It would be a great consolation for my mother, for my wife, for my children, for my brothers, for my relatives, even for my protectors, for my countrymen." His speech was a review of all the events in the Northwest since 1869, the failure of the government to listen to the Métis and their grievances, its failure to grant him the promised amnesty, and his long exile.

When he had finished, Judge Richardson passed sentence. "Louis Riel," he said, "you have been found by a jury . . .

guilty of a crime the most pernicious and greatest that man
can commit. . . . For what you have done the law requires
you to answer. . . . It is now my painful duty to pass the
sentence of the court upon you, and that is that you be taken
now from here to the police guard-room at Regina . . . that
on the 18th of September next you be taken to the place
appointed for your execution, and there be hanged by the
neck till you are dead."

Riel had been condemned to death, but would he go to the
gallows? Would the sentence be carried out? Would the jury's
recommendation of mercy save him? According to a Winnipeg newspaper, every juror had been heard to say after the
trial that while they were obliged to render a verdict of guilty,
yet they sympathized with Riel and the Northwest agitation.
Another newspaper reported that three of the jurors said the
meaning of their recommendation was that Riel should not
be hanged. One of the jurors wrote to a friend (the letter was
later read in Parliament) saying that in recommending Riel to
the mercy of the court they did not wish to justify rebellion. At the same time they believed that, had the government done its duty and redressed the grievances of the
halfbreeds, there never would have been a rebellion.*

From all parts of Canada, the United States, Britain, and
France, petitions were sent to the government requesting
clemency. In Quebec, French Canadians were aroused and
demanded a pardon for Riel, while in other parts of the
country people were determined that the execution should

* In 1925 one of the jurors, Edwin J. Brooks, said: "We were in a dilemma. We
could not pass judgement on the Minister of the Interior, who was not on trial;
and we had to give our finding on Riel according to the evidence. We refused to
find him insane. The only thing we could do was to add the clause to our verdict
recommending mercy. We knew it wasn't much, but it was not an empty formal
expression and it expressed the serious desire of every one of the six of us."

be carried out. A racial and religious storm was developing and many thought that it could destroy Confederation.

At first Macdonald did not think the storm would amount to much. But as the passions in Quebec and Ontario became more heated, he had difficulty in holding his cabinet together. What was he to do? Should he pardon Riel to satisfy Quebec or let him hang to please English Canada? If he did not pardon Riel, would his French-Canadian cabinet ministers continue to support him? Quebec demanded that if the cabinet could not agree on a decision to pardon Riel, the French-Canadian ministers should resign. Moreover, if the decision was to let Riel hang, Macdonald had to consider whether the French-Canadian Conservatives in Parliament would continue their support.

On September 17, after his mother and some of his family had visited Regina to say farewell to him, Riel learned that his execution had been postponed; a new date had been set while an appeal was being considered by a higher court. His inner strength dissolved when he heard the news and he began to sob hysterically. Later he wrote to his mother, convinced it had been his family's prayers that had won him this reprieve. "Thus", he said, "I have twenty-nine more days to prepare myself for death, and to enjoy life." In October another reprieve was granted so that an appeal could be made to the Judicial Committee of the Privy Council in London. There was still another when Macdonald, under pressure from his French-Canadian colleagues, agreed to appoint a medical commission to consider Riel's mental condition. Their opinion was the same as that of the doctors at the trial: on subjects other than religion and politics Riel was able to distinguish between right and wrong. Dr Jukes, however, wrote a letter to Macdonald saying that he would be pleased if public opinion could be satisfied without taking Riel's life. Nevertheless Macdonald made up his mind that the execution could be postponed no longer. The date was to be November 16.

During these months of waiting Riel filled notebooks with prayers and prophecies. Still fighting for his cause and that of the Métis people, he wrote to the American Consul in Winnipeg suggesting that a Canadian-American commission be set up to investigate the claims of the Indians and the halfbreeds. He wrote to United States President Grover Cleveland, outlining the wrongs he said had been committed by the Canadian government against the people of the Northwest and suggesting that the United States annex the country. And there were letters to his mother and his wife bidding them to have courage and to pray for him. "My dear Mother," he wrote, "I thank you and I can never thank you enough for having raised me in the recognition and service of God. I thank you for the blessings you have given me and that you continue to bring me by your devout life . . . may my children and the children of my children . . . cherish your name forever."

Michael Lavell, the doctor at Kingston Penitentiary who was one of the medical commission appointed by Macdonald to examine Riel, described him at this time:

Louis Riel was physically well developed and in his prime when I saw him early in November 1885—manly expression of countenance, sharp eyes, intelligent and pleasing address. His conversational powers were remarkable, voice capable of any amount of modulations with a rare charm about it. At times in conversation he maintained all the characteristics of his race, excitable and enthusiastic, while at other times, when speaking of circumstances having reference to his pres-

ent position and prospects, his voice was soft, mellow and sweet, interesting to a degree, drawing out the sympathies of the listener.

During the last days in his cell at Regina, Riel showed no fear of death. More than anything else he was worried about his family—his wife and children, his mother—and the disgrace brought on them by his execution as a criminal. He did not want his children to grow up ashamed of their father. Even as this concern pained him, one sorrow seemed to pile upon another. His wife was ill—dying of tuberculosis. Then in October she gave birth to a second son, who lived for only a few hours. "The misery that I feel in seeing my little one taken from me," he wrote to his sister Henriette, "without ever being able to embrace him, without ever being able to give him my love, strikes me to the innermost depths of my soul."

While Riel waited in jail, the storm that had risen in Canada over his fate was gathering force. Feelings had reached the point of fanaticism as English-speaking Canadians demanded that he be hanged and French Canadians acclaimed him as a hero. As the day of the execution approached, demands for vengeance on the "murderer" and "traitor" were echoed by cries of justice and mercy for the "saint" and "martyr".

Macdonald had to make a choice. He chose not to interfere with the sentence of death imposed by the court.

When he was told there would be no further reprieve, Riel was calm. He was resigned to his fate. Late on November 15 he wrote his last letter to his mother: "May you be blessed", he said, "from generation to generation for having been so good a mother to me. . . . It is two hours past midnight. Good Father André told me this morning to hold myself la souffrance.

Je vous embrasse tous avec la
plus grande affection.

Vous chère maman, je vous embrasse
un doit faire un fils dont l'âme est
pleine d'amour filial.

Vous ma chère épouse, je vous embrasse comme doit le faire un
époux chrétien, selon l'esprit catho-
lique de l'union conjugale.

Mes chers petits enfants, je vous embrasse comme doit le faire un
père chrétien, en vous bénissant
selon l'étendue de la miséricorde
divine, pour la vie présente et pour la vie future.

Vous, mes chers frères, et sœurs,
beaux frères et belles sœurs, neveux
et nièces, parents, proches et amis,
je vous embrasse avec tous les bons
sentiments dont mon cœur est capable.

Soyez tous heureux. — chère maman,
Je suis votre fils affectueux
suis et obéissant   Louis "David" Riel.

The conclusion of Riel's last letter to his mother, in which he says farewell to her, to his wife, his children, his brothers, sisters, nephews, and nieces ready for tomorrow. I listen to him, I obey. I am prepared for everything. . . . But the Lord is helping me to maintain a peaceful and a calm spirit. . . . I am doing everything I can think of to be ready for any eventuality, keeping myself in an even calm. . . . Yesterday and today I have prayed God to strengthen you and grant you all his gentle comfort so that your heart may not be troubled by pain and anxiety."

November 16 was a clear and chilly day. Riel had spent the night in prayer and devotions with his confessor, Father André. At seven o'clock extreme unction was administered. At eight the deputy sheriff appeared at his door. "I am glad to go," Riel said, "and to be relieved of my sufferings." The sheriff asked him if he had any wishes about the disposal of his personal belongings. Riel put his hand on his heart and said: "I have only this. I was willing to give it to my country fifteen years ago, and it is all I have to give now. . . . I have made my peace with God and I am as prepared now as I can be at any time. You will see that I had a mission to perform."

Then Riel—dressed in a black coat, a woollen shirt, grey tweed trousers, and mocassins—with two priests, two guards, and the deputy sheriff, walked in procession from the cell up a flight of stairs to an exit leading to the scaffold. Riel and the priests knelt while Father André recited the Litany. Riel responded in a firm voice. When the prayers were completed Riel stood up and was kissed by the priests. He said to Father André: "I thank God for having given me the strength to die well. I am on the threshold of eternity and I do not want to turn back. I die at peace with God and man, and I thank all those who helped me in my misfortunes."

He showed no sign of weakness as his hands were bound, and he walked calmly to the scaffold and onto the drop while the two priests prayed constantly. "I ask forgiveness of all men," Riel said. "I forgive all my enemies." The executioner drew a white cap over his head. "Courage, Father," he said to André, who was weeping. With the second priest Riel said the Pater Noster. In mid-prayer the trap was sprung.

Four weeks after his execution Riel's body was sent home with an armed guard in a CPR box-car. On the evening of December 11 friends came to his mother's house to pay him homage while the bell of the little church at St Vital rang sombrely. The closing of the casket next morning was watched by Riel's mother and sisters and his wife Marguerite and the two children.* Then, in many sleighs and carriages, the funeral procession set off on the snow-covered road for St Boniface. Inside the cathedral, which was draped in black and filled with mourners from St Boniface and Winnipeg, the casket was placed on a catafalque surrounded by lighted candles. In the presence of Archbishop Taché and the abbé Ritchot a requiem mass was sung.

An old man once recalled the scene when the burial took place in the grounds outside: "I saw people cry. I saw men cry. . . . Everybody was in black."

Their daughter, who was then two, died at the age of eight; their son died at twenty-one.

Epilogue

On November 16 in Toronto crowds gathered outside the newspaper offices waiting for news to be placed on the bulletin boards. When they read of Riel's courage on the scaffold they expressed admiration and then dispersed quietly. But in Montreal the City Council adjourned its meeting in protest at what it called a violation of all the laws of justice and humanity. Portraits of Riel appeared in the store windows and effigies of Macdonald and his French-Canadian colleagues who had supported him were burned in the street. Hundreds of students paraded through the city shouting "Glory to Riel!" Newspapers called on the people of Quebec not to forget that Riel had been tried by an English-speaking judge and jury and then "murdered".

The demonstrations in the street carried over into a bitter agitation against Macdonald's Conservative government and English-speaking Canada—in the newspapers, in public gatherings, and in Parliament. As their province mourned Riel, French Canadians cried out: "Why is Riel dead? Why? Because he was French." In its anguish French Canada put the blame for Riel's death on the racial and religious prejudices of English Canada and began to question whether Confederation, which had joined English and French peoples in a political compact, could survive.

The emotionally charged atmosphere that followed the execution of Riel reached a climax in a great public gathering at the Champ de Mars in Montreal on November 22, 1885.

That day, at an open-air meeting attended by nearly fifty thousand people, Honoré Mercier, the Liberal leader in Quebec, demanded that those guilty of Riel's death be punished. "Riel, our brother, is dead," he cried, "victim of his devotion to the cause of the Métis whose chief he was, a victim of the fanaticism of Sir John and his friends; of the betrayal of three of our own people who, to maintain their cabinet posts, have sold their brother. . . . In killing Riel, Sir John has not only struck at the heart of our race but especially at the cause of justice and humanity which . . . demanded mercy for the prisoner of Regina, our poor friend of the North-West."

Another speaker that day was Wilfrid Laurier. Like others he accused Macdonald and the Conservative government of ignoring the petitions of the Métis—a people, he charged, who had suffered "gross injustice". If he had lived in the Saskatchewan country, he said, he too would have shouldered a musket to fight against the neglect of the government.

Though he was indignant at the execution of Riel, Laurier would not support Mercier's proposal that French Canadians withdraw from both the Conservative and Liberal parties and organize a French-Canadian political party. "We are a new nation," he said, "we are attempting to unite the different conflicting elements which we have into a nation." Mercier's proposal was "suicidal"; it would destroy Confederation by dividing the country politically along racial lines, for English-speaking Canadians would respond by organizing an English-speaking party.

Laurier blamed the Conservative newspapers for inflaming the racial and religious passions of the country. He might well have criticized newspapers of both parties, as well as English and French zealots, who used the death of Riel to attack one another. The execution had aroused extremists on both sides.

It was a critical testing time for the young Confederation. To French Canadians, Confederation had been a compact into which they entered hesitantly in the belief that it would ensure their survival as a minority. In 1885 their uncertainty was aroused again. With the death of Riel they believed that an English-speaking majority in the nation had imposed its will on the government. Their voice had been ignored. Would it be given consideration in the future or would they always find that in any issue dividing the country along racial lines they would have to sacrifice their viewpoint in the face of majority opinion? The fate of Riel in his struggle for the Métis people was to French Canadians a symbol of their minority position in the nation.

A simple explanation of Riel's fate is to say that he was the victim of the politicians who used him to attack one another for party purposes. In this view John A. Macdonald callously weighed the votes he would gain in English-speaking Canada against those he would lose in Quebec. Even Laurier, who had spoken in defence of Riel and Métis grievances, admitted in 1874 that he and his friends in Quebec "took this Riel question & kindled the enthusiasm of the people for him & his friends, in order to damage the old [Conservative] administration who were doing nothing for their relief."

It would be easy to censure calculating politicians and over-zealous newspaper editors for the extreme positions they took. But these men merely reflected the age in which they lived: they played on the emotions of a society that readily responded to religious and racial appeals. The explanation of the Riel tragedy must go beyond this. It lies in the complexities of human behaviour, of the dual Canadian society, and of Riel himself.

Bibliography and Further Reading

As the number of quoted passages in this book suggests, there is a great deal of contemporary material on Louis Riel and his times. Riel himself left behind many manuscripts, which can be found in the Riel Papers in the Manitoba Archives, Winnipeg, and the Public Archives of Canada in Ottawa. Alexander Begg, who went to the Red River Settlement in 1867, kept a journal during the troubles of 1869-70 and this, with thirty-two other documents, is given in *Alexander Begg's Red River Journal and Other Papers Relative to the Red River Resistance of 1869-1870* (Toronto, 1956), edited for the Champlain Society by W. L. Morton; passages from it are quoted in Chapters 2 and 3. Among the useful and illuminating documents in this volume is a translation of Louis Schmidt's memoirs for the period 1868-70; the complete "Memoires" was published in *Le Patriot de l'Ouest* in 1912. Other quotations in these chapters are from the books of C. A. Boulton, *Reminiscences of the North-West Rebellions* (Toronto, 1886), and W. F. Butler, *The Great Lone Land* (London, 1872). Books by others who were involved in the Riel troubles are G. H. Young, *Manitoba Memories* (Toronto, 1897) and C. P. Mulvaney, *The History of the North West Rebellion of 1885* (Toronto, 1885), from which a passage is quoted in Chapter 6.

On the subject of Riel's mental illness, which is described in Chapter 4, use was made of a paper by Olive Knox—"The Question of Louis Riel's Insanity", published in the *Papers of the Historical and Scientific Society of Manitoba* (Series III, No. 6, 1951)—in which quotations from the manuscripts of Dr Gabriel Nadeau, among other contemporary sources, are brought to light and interestingly used. (The description of Riel by Dr Lavell in Chapter 7 is from this paper.) John Lee's recollections of Riel's mental disturbances, published in *La Presse,* 29 April 1886, are also quoted.

The quotation in Chapter 4 from Riel's poem, "To Sir John A. MacDonald", translated by John Glassco, is from a fuller extract included in *The Poetry of French Canada in Translation,* edited by Mr Glassco (Oxford University Press, Toronto, 1970).

Gabriel Dumont's lively recollections of Riel and the battles at Duck Lake, Fish Creek, and Batoche were dictated and transcribed in December 1888. Quotations from this translation by Professor G. F. G. Stanley, which can be found complete in the *Canadian Historical Review* (September 1949) under the title "Gabriel Dumont's Account of the North West Rebellion, 1885", are used in Chapters 6 and 7. The description of Riel by General Frederick Middleton in Chapter 7 is from his *Suppression of the Rebellion in the North West Territories of Canada 1885;* first published in the *United Service Magazine,* November 1893, it was edited by G. H. Needler and republished in 1948.

Other contemporary sources are the journal of Father Ritchot, which can be found translated in W. L. Morton, *Manitoba: The Birth of a Province* (Winnipeg, 1965); Alexander Begg, *The Creation of Manitoba: or, a History of the Red River Troubles* (Toronto, 1871); the Taché letters, found in the Archives de l'archevêche, St Boniface; various newspapers of the time; Canada: Journals of the House of Commons 1874 (Vol. 8, Appendix 6), *Report of the Select*

Committee on the Causes of the Difficulties in the North-West Territory in 1869-70; Canada: Sessional Papers 1870 (Vol. 5, No. 12), *Correspondence and Papers Connected with Recent Occurrences in the North-West Territories;* and Canada: Sessional Papers 1886 (Vol. 19, No. 43c): *The Trial of Louis Riel.*

Any writer on Riel and his times must acknowledge a large debt to Professor G. F. G. Stanley and I am glad to do this here. For his *Louis Riel* (Toronto, 1963) Professor Stanley made a thorough examination of all the sources and presented his findings in a definitive biography. His *The Birth of Western Canada: A History of the Riel Rebellions* (London, 1936; rev. ed. 1960) is another valuable work.

Two other modern books on Riel are Joseph Howard, *Strange Empire: A Narrative of the Northwest,* and E. B. Osler, *The Man Who Had to Hang* (Toronto, 1961). A collection of documents edited by Hartwell Bowsfield, *Louis Riel: Rebel of the Western Frontier or Victim of Politics and Prejudice?* (Toronto, 1969), presents both contemporary and modern statements about Riel and further source material.

Louis Riel has been the subject of an interesting and effective play, *Riel* (1962), by John Coulter and an opera, *Louis Riel,* by Harry Somers, with a libretto by Mavor Moore in collaboration with Jacques Languirand. It was first performed in 1967.

INDEX

17-20; in Montreal, 19-22, 32; returns to St Boniface, 22; opposes surveys, 34-5; before Council of Assiniboia, 35-7; Bill of Rights, 38-9, 43, 54, 56; takes Fort Garry, 40; establishes Provisional Government, 40, 43; captures Portage party, 46-7; and Thomas Scott, 48-51, 88-9; and Manitoba Act, 57-8; appearance, 59, 70, 86, 133; flees from Fort Garry, 60-1; and Fenians, 64-6; reward for, 66; elected to Parliament, 68, 70, 73; in Ottawa, 69, 70; in Plattsburg, N.Y., 69; in Keeseville, N.Y., 69, 73, 78; signs parliamentary register, 70; in Washington, 73, 74-7; mental illness, 75, 76-8, 139, 141, 143; in St Joseph, 80-1; in Manitoba, 82-5, 91-3; marries, 82; becomes an American citizen, 85; revisits Manitoba, 85-91; petitioned to return to North Saskatchewan country, 92-3; and Indians, 101, 123-4; returns to North Saskatchewan, 104-5; establishes Provisional Government, 116; forms Exovedate, 116; at Duck Lake, 119-22; at Fish Creek, 126; at Batoche, 130, 132; surrender, 133; trial of, 136-45; addresses the jury, 140-1, 144; verdict, 144; sentence, 144-5; execution, 150-1; funeral, 151; reactions to execution of, 152-4

Riel, Louis, the Elder, 9, 16, 17, 18, 19, 74
Riel, Marguerite Monet, 82, 104, 113, 133, 134, 148
Riel, Marie Angélique, 82, 151
Riel, Sara, 18, 92
Ritchot, N.J., 43, 54-7, 64, 79, 151
Robinson, Christopher, 143
Robinson, Henry, 49
Ross, James, 38
Roy, François, 78, 139

St Andrew's, 27
St Boniface, 9, 13, 14, 22-3

St Boniface Cathedral, 9, 34
St Joseph, 61, 67, 80
St Laurent, 115
St Norbert, 33, 35, 62
St Paul, 25, 29, 40, 67, 73
St Vital, 35, 63, 85-90
Sayer, William, 16
Schmidt, Louis, 18, 19, 23, 40, 105
Schultz, J.C., 32, 39, 40, 45-6, 52, 54-5, 67
Scott, A.H., 43, 54, 55
Scott, Thomas, 30, 45, 48-51, 55, 56, 61, 71, 88-9, 134, 137
Selkirk, Lord, 11-12, 13
Semple, Robert, 13, 16
Seven Oaks, 13, 16
Simpson, George, 14
Sinclair, James, 16
Smith, Donald A., 41-5, 47-8, 49, 51, 66, 114
Snow, John A., 29-30, 33
Stewart, James, 60
Strange, T.B., 125, 133
Sun River, 104
Sun River Sun, 104
Sutherland, Hugh, 45-6, 47

Taché, Alexandre, 17-18, 23, 29, 33, 60, 61, 62, 64, 67, 89, 151
Thom, Adam, 16
Toronto, 55, 124, 152
Tourond, Calixte, 126, 127, 129

Union Métisse de St Joseph, 111

Wallace, James, 139
Walters, Henry, 116
Walters and Baker store, 116
Wandering Spirit, 123
Washington, 73, 74-7
Winnipeg, 27, 81
Winnipeg Daily Sun, 84
Wolseley, Garnet, 58, 59, 60, 104, 124

Young, (Capt.) George, 134
Young, (The Rev.) George, 48-9
Young, John, 56

CANADIAN LIVES

A series of well-illustrated and lively brief biographies that emphasize character, anecdote, and social history — often by means of vivid extracts from contemporary sources — while giving a clear summary of the main historical events and achievements.

LOUIS RIEL

The rise and fall of Louis Riel (1844-85) spanned only fifteen years, yet he is one of the most controversial and colourful people in our history. The central figure in two rebellions, which he led on behalf of the French-speaking halfbreeds called Métis, has caught the imagination of Canadians few other historical personalities have do His career began with the acts of resistance at the Red River Settlement in 1869, and continued through the formation of a Provisional Government and the notorious shooting of Thomas Scott in 1870, through of mental illness and exile in the United S to the North West Rebellion of 1885. It re an inevitable climax with his surrender an trial and the passionate outpouring of fee that rocked the country when he was foun guilty of treason and executed. The religio and racial emotions of the time, the bigot and opportunism of politicians, and Riel's unstable mental condition all combine to of his life a Canadian tragedy, one that ha profound consequences for Confederatio Hartwell Bowsfield has skilfully condense these events — while quoting generously from letters, books, journals, and other contemporary documents — to present a well-rounded portrait of one of Canada's authentic folk heroes and an absorbing narrative of western history.

HARTWELL BOWSFIELD was born in Toronto and educated in Ontario and Manitoba. He is a gradu of the University of Manitoba and was Provincial Archivist of Manitoba from 1952 to 1967. He is no lecturer in the history of the Canadian West at Ye University and University Archivist. Mr Bowsfield edited *The Letters of James Wickes Taylor: 1859-* (1968) and a book of readings, *Louis Riel: Rebel o the Western Frontier or Victim of Politics and Prejudice?* (1969). He has also compiled two Jack Selkirk and Laurier.

ISBN 0-19-540182-4
Oxford University Press